Introduction

How did we end up in this mess? Did we ever have anything in common? I'm not sure I can take any more fighting. Is it even possible to fix this relationship?

Should I leave him?

If you're having thoughts like these, you're at a crossroads in your relationship. What happened to the good old days, when you met or married your partner? You two seemed perfect for each other and you wanted to spend the rest of your life with him. You laughed, you squabbled, you had great make-up sex. You wanted to be together all the time. He thought you were terrific and you couldn't imagine life without him.

But over the last few years, things have changed. There are fewer laughs, more fights, less sex. The magic has disappeared. It's not *all* bad, but it's not great anymore, either. Some days, you and your partner go through the everyday routines of life and it seems pretty normal (*I could keep doing this*). Then something will trigger a fight (*Is it really THAT difficult to put dirty clothes in the hamper?*) and the snippy argument commences (*I wouldn't have to nag if you just did it yourself!*) and the uncomfortable feelings return (*Another fight? I can't live like this. I hate him! Are we really arguing about dirty clothes, or something bigger?*).

Did he change? Did you change? Who knows? What you do know is that the relationship is not working for you anymore. And you have no clue how to solve the problems, or if you even want to. You're not sure what to do. You may have friends who tell you he's not good enough for you and you need to leave. Your relatives—particularly the older ones—might urge you to hang in there. Marriage is hard, they say, and it's supposed to be tough.

Does it seem like you know so many other couples who are happy? They have healthy relationships, and you want what *they* have. You want to go through life with a partner at your side, not dreading coming home to a battleground. But does your current partner want to end the war and create lasting harmony? Or do you need to run up the white flag, split the assets, and call it quits?

Make no mistake about it; these decisions are not easy. But they become more manageable when you can calmly assess your situation and look objectively at why your relationship has unraveled. That's where this book comes in. As a licensed professional counselor, I help women every day to decide whether to stay or go. In this book, I've compiled my decades of experience into a toolbox of information, quizzes, reflective questions, and stories of other couples just like you. We'll first evaluate your current relationship and sort through your conflicted feelings so you can come to a healthy, informed decision. Part I walks you through analyzing your current relationship. Part II gives you tips on ways you try to fix this relationship. If these don't work, Part III offers strategies to help you move on. Depending on what's right for your situation, you can read to learn strategies either for working it out or for leaving him. No matter which resolution you choose, you'll be more knowledgeable, emotionally stronger, and confident about your future.

Remember, relationships should be a source of great joy and fulfillment, and both of you deserve to feel that way.

where do you stand now?

chapter one

What Does a Good Relationship Look Like?

Things to Consider

- What's good for you?
- What's good for the children? (Don't believe it's always better for the children for you to stay together.)
- What's good for him?

When you're facing problems in a relationship, it's easy to forget what a healthy partnership looks and feels like. Yet it's important to understand the foundations of a happy relationship in order to objectively and effectively evaluate your own relationship at this point. Good, strong relationships come in all shapes and sizes, but they have several things in common:

- **Communication:** Both partners talk about what's bothering them. Disagreements don't have to mean ugly yelling matches. Both partners can express feelings without confrontation. One person may initiate a sit-down conversation, in which each party tells the other what is troubling him or her and together they come up with ways to solve the problem.

- **Trust:** Partners can rely on the other's word and feel secure knowing that the other person is loyal and reliable in all areas of life—financially, physically, and emotionally.
- **Honesty:** Both partners tell the truth, even when one has done something wrong. Partners show each other different perspectives. If one asks, "Do I look fat?" he or she can expect an honest, but loving, response.
- **Compassion and love:** Partners are there for each other. They want to make the other person happy and do little things to show love and appreciation.
- **Commitment:** Partners want to grow old together—they can envision spending the little and big moments together for the rest of their days. They have outside friends, but for both their partner is the center of their world.

Clearly, not every healthy relationship is perfect *all* the time. Even happy couples have disagreements and go through rough times, but they can always return to these basic principles to solve problems and reconnect.

Quiz: Your Current Situation

Now that you have an idea of what makes up a good relationship, take this simple quiz to gauge the health of your relationship.

On a scale of one to five (with one meaning you disagree strongly and five meaning you agree strongly), answer the following questions:

1. Was he ever your best friend? ____4____
2. Have you been together quite a while, and do you have a hard time envisioning your life without him? ____4____
3. Do you sometimes still enjoy one another? ____4____

4. Do you fear you can't make it financially without him?

_____1_____

5. Are you better off with the two of you staying together?

_____3_____

If you scored 20–25 points: This relationship has been good, but isn't working now.

If you scored 11–19 points: You've got reasons to go and reasons to stay . . . but the decision still isn't easy.

If you scored 5–10 points: You've had problems with this relationship for some time, but the fact that you're still here means you need to ponder how this is working for you.

If you're reading this book, you most likely scored in the 11 or more range. In the following few chapters, we'll evaluate the reasons why people stay, as well as why it can be worth it to work things out, rather than leaving.

This quiz may have helped you get an overview of where you stand. Some relationships are in need of a complete overhaul before you can find happiness. In these cases, both partners need to commit to counseling to help resolve the issues in their relationship.

This Isn't Easy, But You're Not Alone

Sometimes women stay in unhappy relationships for all the wrong reasons, such as fear or comfort. Even if your relationship is bad, it's familiar and therefore better than potential future bad relationships in which everything is unknown.

Deciding to either stay or leave is a personal decision that only you can make after you've explored all options. Whether you stay and work on the problems in your relationship or decide it's best to leave him behind, make sure your life works for you. The decision you make will be one of the toughest in your life, and the complete assessment this book offers will help you limit the second-guessing.

Never think you're alone in this. Lots and lots of other women face the same dilemma.

Recognizing Real Love

You might feel as if the man you're with *does* love you, even if the two of you aren't particularly happy. What is your definition of love? Make sure your understanding of the word is accurate. Real love is more than having affectionate feelings every now and then for a man. It's more than hearts and flowers and that giddy feeling you had when you first met. After the honeymoon, real love requires commitment to the well-being and happiness of the other person while maintaining your own self-worth. Love fosters the well-being of the loved one.

If you want to keep this relationship, make sure you are doing your part.

Love feels like this:

- He helps you be a better person.
- His strengths complement yours.
- He likes you and enjoys your company.
- Being with him doesn't mean you sacrifice your self-worth.
- He likes the *best* you—the person you are when you're firing on all cylinders.

If your current relationship doesn't measure up to this standard, maybe you're staying for the wrong reasons. Also, consider whether or not any part of you still *likes* him. This can be difficult to assess. If there's been a lot of strife between you or if you've fallen into very poor communication patterns, you can feel pretty estranged. You may have forgotten how you felt for one another in the beginning. So, is there any "liking" left?

You can have love in a relationship and still not want to stay to work on it, but liking another person has a dangerous allure and can mask more serious problems. Liking another person—enjoying being together, enjoying him laughing at your jokes—can provide just enough connection to keep you in an unhappy relationship even if you've been frustrated a long time. The good news is, if you still like your partner, you have a good basis from which to work on this relationship and deal with your issues.

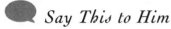 ### Say This to Him
"We both deserve to be happy. I'm evaluating where I am in this relationship."

Relationships are one of the most difficult challenges human beings face, but these connections sustain individuals. According to a research study reported in 2006 by the University of California, Los Angeles, being in a relationship can even prolong your life. In order to build a strong, lasting connection, both partners need to change the behaviors that are getting in their way. Both partners have to learn what they need from each other to be happy and keep the communication open.

Stella's Story:

Mack and I met in college, and we were a couple for three years before we got married. I loved his laid-back manner and that he was calm when I got in a tizzy. We've gone through a lot together. Since we started dating, Mack's brother died when a van hit his motorcycle, and my parents divorced, to my total surprise. Despite Mack having dropped out of school, he was with me when I finally graduated college and started teaching. Lately, though, things have been tense. A year ago, we had a baby and stuff just started to pile up on us. Mack seemed more distant as he struggled to get adjusted to his new role as dad. Although he makes good money, he doesn't like his job and he wants to go back to school. I know I'm sometimes difficult to live with, but I was still shocked when a night of drinking with his buddies led Mack into an "almost-infidelity." I was just blind-sided.

He confessed and told me about the whole situation, but my faith in our relationship is shaken. I've tried my best to understand his confusion and unhappiness, but I still wonder if I can trust him again. Sometimes, I think I hate him, but I still can't quit loving him, either. My friends tell me that I should leave him, that "once a cheater, always a cheater." But I'm not sure it's that cut-and-dried.

We're in a bad situation, and I don't know how to make it better. I can't forget him making out with another girl. I know his drinking that night is partly to blame for him getting with that girl, and it was probably partly because he's been upset about his work. But I don't know how to make him happy all the time. Is he going to cheat again? Should I just say that he can never go out unless I'm there? We keep arguing about this and we're struggling to move forward. He didn't actually have sex with that girl, but that doesn't make me feel better.

Because she still loves him, Stella needs to explore every avenue before giving up on this relationship. She and Mack need to seek counseling to sort out the relationship or try relationship seminars to help them learn how to better communicate. To avoid any future incidences of infidelity, Mack should develop an awareness of, and better ways to deal with, his emotional struggles. Stella needs to see that she doesn't listen and actually has made it easy for him not to talk to her. Mack has to learn to handle his frustrations differently. His kissing another woman is in no way Stella's fault, but if she stays with him, she has to become more aware of his struggles.

You know you love him when it's really important to you that he prospers, and when you really hate the idea of him doing it with someone else. Be realistic. If you leave him, you're out of his life. Don't think you still get input through being his "friend."

Fixing It Requires . . .

If the two of you have a basis for a relationship and you want to move forward in a resolved, happy manner, there are some things you'll need to do. Many relationships have potential, but the partners don't realize this because they have become too polarized—you're strongly convinced that you're right in your own view of issues, just as your partner is solid on his perspective being correct. Being on opposite ends of the spectrum can make for a balanced relationship, but only if you understand and value the other side. Respecting your partner's point of view and the way he sees the problem can lead to enlightenment in the way you deal with issues and help to balance you as an individual.

> ### Good Reasons to Stay
> - You two share a whole lot of "liking."
> - You both have a willingness to do the difficult work— communication, compromise, and so on.
> - You have a good relationship foundation.

In order to find this kind of appreciation for one another, you'll need to be less defensive about your own perspective and less threatened by your partner seeing things differently. Being defensive can be fueled by negative comments from your partner, but also by your own self-doubt. Take a step back, try to turn off the emotion, and logically look at his comments and your reaction to them. When individuals are confident in themselves, they usually don't need to defend themselves.

You Have Immense Personal Power

You are fully equipped to deal with the sometimes frustrating, sometimes glorious moments in life all by yourself, even if you don't feel capable of doing so. It may be hard to believe this right now, but you are a strong individual who is in control of your destiny.

Regardless of whether you seek another relationship or go it alone, you deserve to be loved and to live in a relationship in which you generally feel loved.

The basis of any good relationship is that each person chooses to be in it. This choice implies personal power, which is critical. You may not feel this power, but realizing you have it is essential to the evaluation process. Once the thought of leaving a relationship has entered your head, it can be hard to dispel. The purpose of this book is to help you evaluate whether or not it's best for you to leave your current relationship. Based on your assessment of it, you need to either become 100 percent committed to fixing the situation or resolve to get out.

Recognize Your Positive Steps

While it may not seem significant, you're making progress simply by deciding to take action. You're actively working to figure out what to do with this relationship. While it probably feels uncomfortable right now, you're moving toward a better place. You should be proud of yourself for making your happiness a priority.

- **You should stay if:** You're both working toward changing the ways you interact.
- **You should leave if:** He's actively working against changing the relationship.

Exercises and Affirmations

Take a walk in a park and BREATHE. Strangely enough, people don't breathe deeply when they're stressed—as you likely are right now. As you do this, focus your mind on the fact that *you can do this*. Even though you sometimes don't feel like it, you're fully capable of having a great relationship. Ask three friends what they think are your strong points. Really listen to their responses. Pay attention to the strong points your friends see in you. Remember them when you doubt your ability to make this tough decision.

Go to the mall or some other busy place, and take a look at the couples there. These people are living their lives together. They aren't perfect, and most of them don't look perfect. They are just regular people like you. Remember that you're not the only person in the world who's dealt with relationship turmoil and change. You can do this. You're just as strong as everyone else.

chapter two

A Relationship Evaluation: Finding Objectivity

Things to Consider

- Did you have big value conflicts with him from the beginning that you just didn't want to see? Now is the time to face those conflicts.
- Do you really even care about his point of view anymore?
- Are you so angry that you can't see his point of view? Even if you don't stay, you need to understand him to some degree.

The purpose of this chapter is to help you assess the issues in your relationship with clarity so you can address them with your mate. Getting a handle on the specifics of your feelings and needs is vital to determining whether the two of you can work out your problems. We'll try to get at the heart of the issues through a series of questions and exercises.

Criteria—What's Important to You

When conducting any kind of evaluation, it's vital to first decide the criteria to measure answers against. This is tricky when evaluating a relationship because emotions can run strong and you have to separate your needs from everyone else's. What's really important in a relationship is a very personal thing because it involves deciding what's most important to you. Not important to your parents or your girlfriends, but to *you.*

When you think about your personal values and what's important to you, remember that:

- They can't be right or wrong (unless, of course, you value something that's against the law!).
- Values can change, but not easily and **never for someone else**, no matter how much you think you love him.

With that in mind, make a list of what you need in your life. These are the things that really matter. Here's a sample list to get you thinking:

- To live in the woods—the quiet helps clear your mind.
- To devote your time to your job. As demanding as it is, you love it.
- To live simply, with few possessions.
- To not have kids.
- To travel as widely as you can.
- To be with someone who respects your values.

Your relationship criteria are the basis for your judgment. Remember, you're making a judgment call here about whether to stay or go. Look at your list and compare it to your life with him. Does the list match your life right now? If not, are the issues so large that you should leave him? You need some way to evaluate this relationship.

Quiz: Do You and Your Partner Agree about Values?

On a scale of one to five (with one meaning you disagree strongly and five meaning you agree strongly), answer the following questions:

1. You're not sure about what your values are and what's truly most important to you. ____1____
2. You can list the three things that are most important to him, and you're not first on the list. _____
3. You're pretty sure that you and he don't have the same values. ____4____
4. He struggles with the same things you struggle with. ____2____
5. You're afraid he—or you—might just be done, finished with the relationship. All that there was to be given, has been given. ____1____

If you scored 20–25 points: This relationship seems deeply divided and you're pretty sure it's over.

If you scored 11–19 points: The core of the relationship needs some work, but you do have some things in common.

If you scored 5–10 points: The two of you have issues that need serious communication.

Disagreeing on core issues puts a massive strain on a relationship. Some of these disagreements can have major consequences—such as whether you have money for retirement or will have reason to celebrate Mother's Day. That's why it's important to face them head-on if you want to try to save the relationship.

Hannah's Story:

Findley and I have only been together three years, but I feel like it's been forever, both in a bad way and in a good way! When we met,

I thought Findley was great, and he is a good person, just maybe not so great for me. Findley's mother was a go-get-'em lawyer who blazed a trail for women's rights and she raised Findley to be kind of an activist. I'm not like that, though, and I've been wondering lately if he'd be happier with a woman more like his mom.

When we first met, I worked at a large retail store, dressing windows. Findley is a lawyer and specializes in defending high-profile cases. We live in very different worlds, and that wasn't a problem in the beginning.

I work and live in Manhattan and I love having a lot of friends and a full social life here in the city. Findley commutes back and forth from New York to Washington, as his case load dictates, and when we started dating, he came as often as he could. At first, he seemed amused by my friends and the sometimes crazy things we do. And he certainly acted like he enjoyed my fashion addiction. He used to laugh and say my friends and I were fun.

I moved into Findley's New York place after we'd been dating only a couple of months and we started a routine together. I worked and hung out with my friends. He flew back and forth to do his lawyer thing. Everything was great, at first, but it's been going bad for a while now. After we'd been going out a few months, he started buying me "issue" books. I thought he just wanted me to know the kind of thing he was doing, but these publications were about things that don't really interest me. He even bought me a book about how the fashion industry fosters dangerous child labor in developing countries. It's not that I'm not against child labor. I just don't want to think about that when I'm trying to get dressed for work.

Then, Findley started suggesting I take various classes to *improve my understanding of issues*, like he thought I didn't get it, or something. I laughed it off at first, telling him I was going to get a complex and think he saw me as shallow. He denied it, of course, but he still didn't stop giving me flyers and more books!

Lately, I'm starting to feel like Findley wants a more serious-type person than me. He doesn't hang out with my friends anymore and, when he does go out to dinner with someone, it's with other do-gooder, lawyer types. I can feel him pulling away and I'm starting to get tired of not being good enough for him.

If these two look seriously at their values, they'll probably find that they have different priorities and different interests. These are the foundation of a relationship, and it's really hard to make a long-term commitment without a foundation. Hannah has a life she's happy with, so Findley needs to ask himself whether he will be happy if this never changes. Hannah also needs to look at the life Findley is crafting and see if what he wants is really want she wants.

Evaluate the Relationship

You probably have moments when you tell yourself it'll be okay. Are you right? Answer this series of **True/False** questions and find out what areas are the most difficult.

Sex! Better Than a Root Canal?

- ❑ Sex used to be fun, but it's now . . . complicated.
- ❑ Kids, work, chores—doing it all and then doing him leaves you feeling tired and unenthused.
- ❑ You have fantasies you're not sure you can share.
- ❑ You have fantasies you're not sure you can share with *him*.
- ❑ You can't get him off the couch long enough to find your pleasure spot.
- ❑ Zero to sixty in a minute and a half.
- ❑ Not enough of it.
- ❑ Too much of it.
- ❑ Having two to tango seems like one too many.
- ❑ Sex with him is about as much fun as cleaning the oven.

If you answered **True** to five or more statements, you're in the normal range. But you want to be better! Broaching this topic can be difficult. It's usually best if you start by talking about how awkward you both feel and how strange it is to feel awkward talking about something you like doing so much! There is the occasional person who doesn't feel weird at all talking about sex, but he or she might not feel so great hearing that some things don't work. And you do need to talk about the things that don't work for you.

Turn to Chapter 4 for more on dealing with conflicts about sex. The key is to clearly communicate what each of you wants.

Start Doing This

Make of list of the big things you and your mate *agree on*. This will take some thought, since it's easier to see disagreements. Keep this list handy and read over it frequently. You need to keep a balance and not think he's all bad.

Bundle of Joy or Bone of Contention?

Answer this series of **True/False** questions to help clarify the areas of conflict you may have with your mate in the realm of parenting.

❑ He insisted you name one of the kids after one of his relatives . . . and you hate the name.

❑ You never really discussed your feelings about having or raising kids.

❑ He's really great at coaching soccer or Little League, but leaves it to you if the kids get sick in the middle of the night.

❑ You've changed more diapers, gotten up more in the night, and made more lunches, but he thinks he knows what's best for the kids.

❑ He's the good guy who gives them what they want, and you
  have to be the enforcer.

❑ You think he's a commandant regarding discipline; he thinks
  you're a marshmallow.

❑ He worries more about consistency and "follow-through" when
  he's trying to improve his golf swing than when it comes to
  child rearing.

❑ He's big on making babies, but not so worried about cleaning
  their spit-up.

❑ When you have disagreements with the kids, he never backs
  you up.

❑ He thinks he's a candidate for Father of the Year when he
  "gives" you an hour for yourself.

If you answered **True** to five or more statements . . . get ready,
you've got work to do. Improvement takes time, but the two of you
need to *bring your A game* for raising the kids. As kids grow older,
parenting gets even more stressful. Work out the issues now.

Children are a common source of relationship conflict. After
all, parenting is one of the most difficult challenges human beings
undertake. Both of you probably have strong feelings about parenting styles, some of them formed from childhood experiences (positive or negative).

Talk about these feelings. See Chapter 4 for more information on
dealing with conflict about parenting. Explain what's important to
you and try hard to listen to what's important to him.

Vacationing from Relationship Issues?

Answer this series of **True/False** questions to see if the two of
you are on the same page about your vacation requirements.

❑ Road trips with him are like a rally race. Fast food only, and no
  bathroom stops.

❑ He's got to see every cathedral and castle. You just want to read a book and lie in the sun.
❑ The only time you really get along is on vacations.
❑ You take great couples' getaways, but always end up fighting about silly things and spoiling the trip.
❑ You always have to visit your in-laws for your vacation. Where's a root canal when you need one?
❑ When on vacations, he spends money you don't have.
❑ One of you likes to plan; the other wants to wander.
❑ You like to splurge on vacation, but he always acts like you're broke.
❑ If he doesn't get sex every night, the vacation is spoiled.
❑ He never wants to take a vacation.

Answering **True** to more than five statements means you've got the vacation blues. It's your vacation, too. Time off from work! Time to bond with your kids. Some couples take vacations to avoid dealing with relationship issues, but most people find stress in the time they'd hoped to de-stress. If you have unresolved issues in your relationship, vacations can stir them up instead of fixing them.

Some couples live for times when they don't have to deal with the conflicts of day-to-day life. When you're staying in a hotel, it doesn't matter if you throw a towel on the bathroom floor, but at home, most people don't have a daily maid to come pick it up. Vacations are just different. You do fun stuff and the two of you might enjoy one another in this brief break from your regular lives.

However, vacations can be hell for some (particularly when you've looked forward to them) if you disagree about how to spend your time. They can also be an opportunity to dodge the issues that already exist between the two of you. If you and your partner work well to resolve conflicts, you'll find a satisfactory resolution that enables you both—possibly at different times—to have enjoyable vacations.

Money Makes the World Go 'Round

Answer this series of **True/False** questions to see if your feelings about money and how it's handled may be causing problems.

❏ You have different ideas about how money should be spent.

❏ Spending money is the biggest fun you share.

❏ You feel like you're competing on *Survivor* . . . against him. It's a fight to the death for the Reward items.

❏ He reminds you of your father—and not in a good way.

❏ About a prenuptial agreement—you wish you hadn't signed it; you wish you had asked for one; you wish you had a better lawyer.

❏ You don't know the family income.

❏ You find out about surprise purchases . . . and not the fun kind (which would be something like a convertible for your birthday, or a week in Maui for the two of you).

❏ It's okay for him to buy golf shoes, but when you buy a pair of strappy sandals, it sets off WWIII. (Not that strappy sandals aren't worth fighting over.)

❏ You don't want to argue about it, so you brush money disagreements under the rug, hoping they'll just go away.

❏ He complains about your spending money, but you think you only buy necessities.

If you answered **True** to more than five statements, it's time to have another money talk . . . yes, one of those. More couples break up over money troubles than any other issue, and money is usually where we play out power and emotional concerns. Have the talk. For more ideas, read the section in Chapter 4 that deals specifically with conflicts about money.

Work/Career

Answer this series of **True/False** questions about how each of your jobs influences your relationship.

- ❑ He spends too much time at work.
- ❑ Relocation seems like a good idea for his career, but is questioned when it's your job that requires the family to move.
- ❑ The kids hardly recognize him.
- ❑ He doesn't see that you have responsibilities that require your time at work.
- ❑ For some reason, he has a lot of after-work "Happy Hours."
- ❑ He always puts you on hold to answer work calls.
- ❑ There are a lot of work calls. (Can a cell phone clog a toilet?)
- ❑ You'd rather be at work than listen to him gripe.
- ❑ To him, his work is a career, while yours is just a job.
- ❑ Your coworkers value you more than he does.

Answering **True** to more than five of the statements means the two of you need to concentrate more on the two of you. If you're like most people, you spend a major portion of your life at work. Don't forget, though, that the ones you love need just as much of your attention.

Getting Out, Going Out . . . Falling Out?

Answer this series of **True/False** questions to see if you're both looking for the same things when you socialize.

- ❑ His idea of a great night out means grabbing dinner at McDonald's.
- ❑ He goes out with his friends every week and leaves you home to entertain yourself.
- ❑ He always wants the two of you to go out alone, without friends.

- ❌ Going out always has to involve alcohol.
- ❏ You can't agree on whether or not it's okay to dance with other people.
- ❏ He thinks you're looking for guys, but you really just want to dance with your girlfriends.
- ❏ It seems like the two of you can't just enjoy each other's company anymore.
- ❏ He doesn't have friends to go out with and can't understand why you want to go out with your friends.
- ❌ He doesn't tell you when he'll be home, then ends up coming in until very late or not until the next day.
- ❌ He hates your best going-out friend and says she's sleazy.

If you answered **True** to five or more statements, you've probably argued about this topic a bunch already. You might be having trouble accepting that you need a different level of socializing than he does. Some people really love grabbing takeout and cocooning all weekend, and only occasionally go out to see a movie. Others crave nightlife. These don't have to be mutually exclusive preferences; different isn't bad. The answer is finding a balance.

Don't succumb to the belief that the two of you just need to socialize separately, though. Having friends and activities that aren't shared by your partner is fine, but if all your recreational time is spent apart and you end up living separate lives, both of you will find decreasing value in the relationship.

 Say This to Him

"I disagree with you on this and I want you to listen to me and respect my opinion, even if you don't agree with me."

Monster-in-Laws

Answer this series of **True/False** questions to see if your families are the source of some of your problems.

- ❑ You don't like his mother and she doesn't like you. At least you have something in common.
- ❑ He doesn't understand why your family celebrates every birthday with a get-together.
- ❑ He calls his brother (or someone else in his family) to complain about you every time the two of you have a fight.
- ❑ He doesn't understand why you talk to your mother so much.
- ❑ Your in-laws think they can tell you how to raise your kids.
- ❑ Your in-laws keep asking you when you're going to have kids.
- ❑ He's always defending your mother when she's crossed the line with you.
- ❑ He comes from a family of losers who always want something from you guys.
- ❑ Your family doesn't like him.
- ❑ You're tired of having to see his family all the time.

Well, maybe they're not monsters, but dealing with in-law conflicts is inevitably tough because they're so personal. If you answered **True** to more than five of these statements, you may need to have a serious discussion before the in-laws get old and your spouse wants them to move in with you. People usually love their families, even when their families haven't given them any apparent reason to do this, so you need to understand his feelings even if you don't agree with them. Turn to Chapter 4 for detailed information on conflicts about family.

Housework—Cold War, Open Hostilities, or Non-Negotiable?

Answer this series of **True/False** questions to see if the two of you see eye to eye on how you keep the house, and who keeps it.

- ❑ You feel like you do everything.
- ❑ His idea of help is to "baby-sit" when you need him to watch the kids.
- ❑ He doesn't even know the chores you hate the most.
- ❑ If he helps at all, he expects applause.
- ❑ If he cooks, you clean. If you cook, you clean.
- ❑ His work stops at five o'clock. You still have all the home stuff to do when you get off work.
- ❑ Laundry—he's a big shot at work, but he can't remember that colors need to be washed in cold water.
- ❑ He keeps mentioning that his mother cooked, cleaned, and worked a full-time job and she didn't feel overwhelmed. You wonder if his old room is still available.
- ❑ He's a pig and doesn't get why you expect him to pick up his underwear.
- ❑ He's a neatnik and gets upset that you don't love doing housework.

Answering **True** to more than five of these statements means you are not on the same page about who does what. Fighting over housework is practically a pastime for a lot of couples. You may find yourself arguing over who does it, when, and how it's done. If one of you channels Martha Stewart and the other couldn't care less if empty soda cans litter the coffee table, there's trouble in relationshipland.

Housework is an unavoidable reality. Even if you don't care about when the clothes get washed or the dishes cleaned, eventually someone's going to have to do it. And that someone will probably do it "wrong" in the eyes of his or her partner.

This is an area in which other relationship issues are often played out (each person's views of gender roles, for example). Don't overlook it. Have a discussion about who's doing what, and when.

Religious War? (And We're Not Talking about the Middle East)

Answer this series of **True/False** questions to see if you both share similar needs and values when it comes to a religious life.

❏ You have a strong religious faith, and that means going to services. He's religious, but he doesn't think attending services is important.

❏ One of you is an atheist, and the other prays about it a lot.

❏ You belong to one religion and he belongs to another.

❏ He hates going to church.

❏ He doesn't like your church.

❏ Your religious differences weren't a problem until you had kids.

❏ You have conflict over how much money/time to give the church.

❏ You don't think kids need to go to church; he does.

❏ He's the Biblical "Head of the Household" unless it's something he doesn't want to deal with.

❏ You're afraid to invite the minister to lunch because your husband might cuss him out.

Having different religious beliefs—especially when it comes to raising kids—can make you feel frustrated, unrespected, and angry. The relationship can get complicated if he doesn't share your beliefs about going to church. Answering **True** to more than five of these statements means you need to have a serious conversation about values. Read Chapter 8 for more information.

Holiday Un-Bliss

Answer this series of **True/False** questions to discover whether your holiday celebrations do more to tear the two of you apart than keep you together.

- ❑ You always visit his relatives for holidays and you're tired of it. Of course, this is better than them coming to your house.
- ❑ He wants to split your holiday time. You feel like all you do is drive.
- ❑ He spends the holidays watching football, while you clean and cook.
- ❑ He doesn't have a clue what you bought the kids this year.
- ❑ Valentine's Day means just a card and grocery store roses, if you're lucky. And then he expects sex. Not that the sex is any better caliber than the roses. . . .
- ❑ You're in charge of all birthday celebrations . . . even your own.
- ❑ He buys you things *he* wants.
- ❑ You're the one buying the gifts for his mother and then he complains about what you choose.
- ❑ When you hear the lyrics to *Blue Christmas* you wonder. . . .
- ❑ It's your job to buy all the gifts, and then he gets upset about how much money you spent.

Sadly, celebrations can bring out the worst in people. If you answered **True** to more than five statements, you might want to have some serious discussion about how you handle holidays—the preparation, the cost, and the way you celebrate them.

Too Many Conflicts May Be Too Much to Deal With

If more than five of these conflict areas resonate with you, you might need to consider leaving. Relationships shouldn't be like living in a war zone. It's reasonable to think you can work out problems in a handful of areas, but if you and your partner have fundamental disagreements about many of these key topics, you are facing a real uphill battle to meet in the middle.

What to Do with Your Evaluation

Now that you have some objective information about the conflicts in the relationship, address these areas with your mate. Remember that you want this discussion to be productive, rather than just have it turn into a gripe session. Pick a time when the two of you can talk without interruption about the areas in which you have the most conflict. Pick only one area to discuss at a sitting, and deal with only those issues. Check out Chapter 4 for more specific information on how to deal with the top five conflicts that couples face.

Practice listening to your mate, as well as how you talk about the conflicts. Both are very important. If nothing seems resolved after your discussion, suggest in a calm manner that the two of you talk to a third party, such as a counselor or some other objective professional who can help you see one another's points of view.

You Can't Be Certain

The truth is that there is no way to know you're making the right decision for you. Maybe after the fact—whether you stay in the relationship now or decide to leave—you'll assess this as a good choice or a mistaken choice. Not now, though. This is a very complicated decision. Knowing which way to jump means you'd be able to see the future and, while there may be some situations that are pretty clear, most aren't.

Still, you need to ask yourself one question: Is it truly the relationship that's causing you problems? Or will your major personal issues be with you still, even if you leave him? Changing a relationship rather than changing yourself doesn't usually result in increased happiness. You contribute at least half of what's happening in this relationship. You will take yourself and your challenges into the next relationship. If you're not happy where you're at, you need to change your self-inhibiting behaviors, as well as insisting he change his. Just jumping out doesn't make everything better. Of course, sometimes leaving a flawed, dysfunctional relationship is a sign of personal growth. If you work on yourself and your partner refuses to change, you might need to leave, even if that's the last thing you want.

Ask yourself—will life be better if you get out? Or will you just find another problem?

Recognize Your Positive Steps

The checklists in this chapter should have helped you pinpoint the main sources of conflict within your relationship. Simply doing this takes courage—you may be admitting things to yourself that you hadn't fully accepted before. In addition, you've put yourself first by identifying what criteria are most important to you. You're making progress just by clarifying the issues. Once you see a problem in glaring, neon lights, it's easier to make decisions on how to handle it.

- **You should stay if:** He's working to see your point of view as hard as you're trying to see his.
- **You should leave if:** He keeps telling you that you're wrong and you should always agree with him (because he's always right, of course).

Exercises and Affirmations

Repeat this mantra several times a day: "I have a right to my own belief system." Do this particularly if your belief system is very different from his.

Make a list of what you think are his core beliefs. Ask him to make his own list and see if you were accurate. You need to see his point of view, too, if you are going to make a solid decision about the relationship.

chapter three

Recognizing Argument Patterns

Things to Consider

- Are you fighting because this seems to be the only way you two talk?
- Are you trying to feel close by arguing about problems just so you can have that "make-up" closeness?
- Are you falling into the repeated arguments because you're trying to make him see your point? Maybe he doesn't want to see it.

Doesn't want to participate as a partner.

Never have time to talk about issues!

Have you noticed that there's a pattern to the arguments you and your spouse have? The subject of the fight gets repetitive, as does everything you two say and how you say it—you hear the same accusations and make the same complaints over and over again. If so, you're not alone. Couples usually argue in a predictable, repetitive way. Some couples even find a kind of comfort in this familiarity, kind of like sitting in the same seat week after week in a classroom. Though you may not recognize it as "comforting," since you are fighting, the sameness can give the conflict a routine that makes it less scary.

Repetition without resolution is like water flowing over stone—it eventually wears you down. Sooner or later, the pointless arguments don't even lead to great make-up sex—they are just yelling matches that leave you exhausted. The fighting may even leave you feeling so battered and angry that you can't stand the thought of being near your mate for quite a while after a disagreement.

Even if you and your partner "never fight," your relationship still has conflict—you just aren't dealing with it openly. Arguing is a necessary part of an intimate relationship. Learning to fight *correctly* is the key to reconnecting and getting the relationship back on track when it derails.

Quiz: How Do You Two Argue?

On a scale of one to five (with one meaning you disagree strongly and five meaning you agree strongly), answer the following questions:

1. You argue over a variety of issues. _____
2. He seems to overreact all the time. _____
3. You talk about how you see things, but you don't think he hears you. _____
4. It seems like you're the one who always *gives in*. _____
5. You try to avoid talking because it never seems to get you anywhere. _____

If you scored 20 or more points: Your fighting styles are very unhealthy and leave both partners feeling worse than when the fight began. You and your partner don't recognize the issues between you and can't communicate about them.

If you scored 11–19 points: You probably resolve some of your fights, but find that some key arguments flare up again and again. They usually end without a tangible solution or agreement.

If you scored 5–10 points: You are likely avoiding problems when they arise.

Disagreements with your significant other can serve a purpose. Working through disagreements in a relationship will help you to see yourself more clearly. You get another point of view, and this can be invaluable. After all, he's been in this relationship with you for a while; he probably has some valid observations about your actions. He actually has a perspective you need to examine. This doesn't mean he's always 100 percent right, but every now and then he's got a point you need to hear. Being able to hear his criticism with an open mind—without reacting and getting mad—can be tough. Step back and examine what he says and try to think about it logically, without emotion. Could he be right?

Can't We Just Stop Fighting Altogether?

It's tempting, but avoiding conflict is a real risk. You'll just sweep problems under the rug rather than face them head-on. While attacking problems is certainly difficult, it's a necessary part of maintaining a healthy relationship. Here are the two main risks of avoiding conflict:

1. **It's dishonest.** If your partner has ever lied to you, or not told you something important, you know that this kind of deceit can have a high cost. The offender may say it's not deceit, but when you're on the other side—in the dark about something— you probably feel deceived.
2. **Problems don't disappear; they snowball.** Conflict avoidance may sound like a good idea, but avoiding problems just delays them until they're bigger and uglier.

Since you can't avoid problems, you need to talk about them. *Talking about issues is the only way to reach a resolution, even though it might not feel good while you're in the middle of it.* This principle is true whether you're going to fix this relationship or enter a new one in the future. The old cliché "it will get worse before it gets better" applies here—talking through a problem is no fun, but it's the only way to resolve it.

Healthy Communication During a Fight

Believe it or not, there *is* a healthy way to fight. The key is to communicate in a respectful and productive way during as much of the fight as possible. Try these tactics:

- **State your position without blaming him or trying to excuse yourself.** In the heat of the moment, separating the problem from your partner can be very difficult. But doing it helps highlight the true source of the conflict rather than attacking your partner (a sure way to get his defenses up immediately). For example, instead of saying, "If you helped *at all* around the house, I wouldn't be so stressed out!" say, "Sometimes I feel overwhelmed by all the responsibilities of the kids, the house, and my job."

- **When he talks about what's upsetting him, "listen" to his emotions.** Some people aren't good at explaining their feelings in words, but their body language or tone of voice may be very telling. For example, instead of saying, "Don't use that tone of voice with me!" say "I know you get upset when it seems like I'm not hearing you."

- **Resist the impulse to explain yourself (over and over).** When you hit this point, your communication is no longer productive; it has dead-ended. If your partner still does not understand your point, find *different* ways to explain the same thing. For example, instead of repeating "I can't *believe* you forgot my birthday!" try listing adjectives that describe how you feel and why: "When you forget my birthday, I feel sad, angry, and disappointed because it's the one day of the year when I want to feel extra special." If your partner does understand your point, he should be able to use the following tactic to show he is on the same page. Then, you can move on with your discussion.

- **Repeat each other's words.** Even if you disagree with how your partner sees things, you can still show him that you understand his concerns. Repeat back to him what he's said so he knows you heard him. And of course, this technique works the other way around, too; he should be able to repeat your words back to you. Follow the instructions in the next section.

 Say This to Him
"I want to hear what you're telling me and I need you to hear me, too."

The Key Communication Method: Listen-and-Repeat

This simple listening technique can solve a number of basic communication problems within a relationship. Just follow these three steps:

1. Tell him you don't think he feels that you're listening.
2. Ask him to tell you what you haven't heard and then do your very best to listen without defending yourself.
3. When he's done talking, repeat back to him what you've heard. Don't just repeat the actual words—try to capture the feelings behind his words as well. Hsurt, uncared for, unimportant— whatever emotions you hear him telling you.

If he tells you that you're wrong, return to Step #2 so he can repeat what he said and you can make another attempt to understand him. Don't be snide or snarky when you do this. If you react in those ways, you won't move toward open communication.

The Benefits of Good Communication

Even if some of these tactics feel silly in the heat of an argument, they help ensure that you and your partner are having a productive fight. You'll truly *hear* what he is saying, you'll notice his *nonverbal* cues, and you'll actually move *through* the fight instead of around and around in the same frustrating circle. Using these tactics doesn't necessarily mean that every fight ends by kissing and making up, of course—but they do help the two of you get to the emotions behind the conflict. When you both feel understood, finding a solution is possible.

Stephanie's Story:

Dave used to walk out on our fights. He'd be angry and just stomp away. Finally, one day I thought I'd try what I learned in my business communication course on settling disputes in the workplace. He was yelling at me that it didn't matter what he said or did, I always had my mind made up already. I really wanted to *explain* myself and defend myself against what felt like unfair accusations, but I gritted my teeth and didn't. I'd said all that before and it only made things worse.

Instead, I tried to talk to him differently. I felt stupid acting like a parrot, but I repeated something he said about how he thinks I don't hear him. It seemed crazy because he'd just said that, but he said yes and actually seemed a little less angry. I felt encouraged then and I repeated all the things he'd been yelling at me. I *had* been hearing him yell these at me, but I guess he didn't think I heard him because he thought I already had my mind made up. It was hard to say all the stuff he'd been telling me, because I didn't agree with most of it, but I wanted him to know that I heard him saying it to me.

Even though this kind of communication seems clunky and awkward and pointless, remember that you're trying to show him that you hear him.

Types of Argument Patterns

At this point, step back and figure out exactly how the two of you disagree in the heat of the moment. What are the specific patterns to your fights? If you can see the way your arguments take shape, you can better decide what needs to change in order to have more of a resolution to your conflicts.

Here are several types of common argument patterns and a brief definition of each:

- **Sniper fire:** When one of you takes shots out of the clear blue sky
- **Full-frontal assault:** Involves name-calling and yelling
- **Gopher:** Pops up and then goes underground again
- **Simmering:** An ongoing argument that exists for a long time because it is never fully dealt with
- **Tag-team:** Where one or both of you involves friends and/or relatives
- **Public:** One or both of you airs grievances in front of others
- **Attack/apologize:** One of you rants and raves, then feels sorry for some of the things said

Sniper Fire

"Sniper fire" is when one partner takes shots at the other out of the blue without saying what's bothering him or her. People who argue in this style usually want to avoid a fight, but instead, hidden anger comes out when it's least expected. You might be convinced that things are good between the two of you and then, *Bam!* out of the blue, your mate takes a shot at you about you never doing the dishes, getting the oil changed in the car, or putting the kids to bed when it's your turn.

If the accusation is said with a shrug or a faint smile, it can feel even worse. You feel attacked and yet your partner acts completely clueless about how hurtful and unexpected the comment is. In this case, you'll probably feel frustrated and won't be sure if you should even be upset. For example, let's say you and another couple are going to an action movie and your partner mentions that you usually never want to see action movies. He loves rough-and-tough movies, as your friends know very well. While action movies might not be your favorite, you know you've never refused to see one with him.

Don't Stereotype by Gender

While jokes abound about the ways women deal with relationship conflicts versus how men do, there are no valid gender stereotypes on this battlefield. Some men insist on full-out fights, while others prefer never to talk about what angers them. It's much more effective to match each of your personalities to an argument pattern rather than to assume you two argue one way or another based solely on your gender.

What's Behind Sniper Fire

Sniper fire can appear at any time in any place, even when you least expect it, and it can be a sign of hidden anger. This can be his unspoken frustration about him wanting sex and you feeling the need to connect with him before jumping into bed, or he might be angry about you nixing the surround-sound setup he wanted.

Beyond a sniper-fire argument style, you or your partner may be showing signs of hidden anger if either of you:

- Refuses sex
- Never has time to spend with the other person
- Chooses to be with friends when being with the other person is an option
- Ignores requests
- Tells the other person he or she is "fine" when that's obviously not the case
- Hides financial information
- Fails to bathe or care for yourself physically (I've actually heard this from clients)
- Knowingly does something to disrupt sleep or make the other person late for work

These forms of attempted communication aren't functional or productive. Nothing about them feels loving, and they just lead to further arguments. Regardless of how you try to explain to him how his action-movie comment upset you, he might steadfastly refuse to acknowledge that he meant anything by it. You *know* he meant something, but because he refuses to admit it, you start feeling like you're overreacting . . . which is, of course, what he now says. You don't want him feeling deprived (after all, he might start sneaking around on you with some girl who *loves* action movies), but it also bugs you that he's made his comment in front of your friends. They'll now think that you're uptight and that the two of you have problems in your relationship. Even if you two *do* have problems, you may not have faced them with one another yet. Suddenly the supposedly "meaningless" comment has snowballed into your feeling that he has a major problem with you.

How to Respond to Sniper Fire
If your partner argues in this way, calmly state your feelings and request that he talk to you about whatever conflict is really prompting the sniper action. Even if he's not immediately aware of what's

upsetting him, you can tell him that it seems as if he's distressed about something and you're interested in knowing what it is. You need to be aware, though, that for this technique to be effective, you have to act like you want to hear his point of view, even though you might be smarting from his attack. Otherwise, he won't tell you about what's bothering him. He'll just continue to "shoot" at you when you least expect it. If you get (understandably) upset at the initial comment and start accusing him of making you look bad in front of your friends, he's probably not going to talk with you openly about what's bothering him.

One thing to realize—no one uses the sniper fire technique if he feels that his partner is really listening to his complaints. Of course, this doesn't mean you're not listening—but if you're being fired on, he's not feeling *heard*. You need to work very hard at hearing what he's trying to tell you, even if you don't think he's listening to you. Someone's got to start, and you'll both feel better if you give this all you've got.

Full-Frontal Assault

This kind of argument has both benefits and liabilities. If you're really angry about something your partner did or didn't do, it may seem very natural to let it all hang out. You're irritated, you're hurt, and you want him to know it. You can probably tell him—in glorious detail—how he's disappointed you and let you down. If he promised to pay a bill and didn't, it can feel like he's lied to you and perhaps even put you in financial jeopardy. (Money issues, as discussed in Chapter 4, are a common source of bitter conflict because they are rooted in fear, power, and security.)

The problem with the full-frontal assault is that it may not be intended as an assault at all. You're just trying to explain how you feel. Your distress over this situation may cause you to raise your voice, but that seems called for, given how upset you are. In a loving relationship, both partners care how the other feels, so he ought to care that you're mad about this. Talking about it is completely reasonable, but *how* you talk to him will help decide whether or not he hears you.

Name-Calling

Do you get so angry that you call your partner names? If this is part of your flawed, dysfunctional communication attempts, you might excuse the behavior because you were so mad. You probably only feel compelled to call him names when it doesn't seem like he's listening to you or really understanding the gravity of the situation, but name-calling doesn't help the two of you understand one another.

Don't Name-Call

Name-calling is the relationship "gateway drug" to worse and worse behaviors. Don't do it. There are better, more effective ways to get your partner to listen.

Name-calling is dysfunctional, and even worse than that, it isn't productive. If you call your significant other a jerk (or more colorful variations), it's probably because you feel like you can't get through to him. It may seem that name-calling is the only way you can get his attention. Still, while calling him a name may let him know you're upset, it also causes him to feel reactive and defensive. In some men, it's like turning off the "hearing" switch. Your mouth is moving, but he's not listening.

Avoiding This Tactic Yourself

Get his attention at a time when he's not watching the playoffs or knee-deep in fixing his car. Don't call names or threaten to leave him. Just tell him how you're feeling. If you're prone to arguing this way, ask yourself these questions:

- **Are you angry and don't feel listened to?** If so, ask your partner what he heard you say and request that he repeat this back to you, as described earlier in this chapter.
- **Do you think he's not understanding how upset you are?** If so, find a way to verbalize your feelings in a concrete way. Rather than point to events ("You're such a jerk for missing my friend's party"), point instead to how you felt when the events happened ("When you didn't show up at the party, I felt miserable, lonely, and embarrassed").

How to Respond to Dysfunctional Arguing Styles

If he is the one who calls names, does it seem like you can't do anything right and the entire relationship has been a disappointment to him? Like you're a disappointment to him? If so, try talking calmly about his feelings. Don't tell him he's wrong to feel whatever he feels; just tell him you know that he's upset and angry and that you want to hear him. After you say this and he calms down some, mention that when he uses ugly names and yells at you, you actually have a harder time listening.

- **Have you had this fight again and again but it still keeps coming up?** If so, ask what he hears you saying. If it's something you're inadvertently saying or something he automatically shifts into when you're mad ("You're upset, so I'm sure you think I did something wrong"), clarify that you both love one another and want to work this out.
- **Did you witness your parents name-calling?** If so, separate yourself from this learned behavior by reminding yourself that it's unproductive and hurtful.
- **Do you feel uncomfortable or unable to talk about your feelings, and it seems easier to verbally attack?** If so, remember that you love this person and need to be able to share openly.

Begin by disclosing that you're not comfortable talking about your feelings.

Knowing why you argue this way will help you choose different communication methods to get your point across.

Gopher Arguments

These kinds of fights resemble gophers in that the argument pops up and then goes underground. The bickering can seem endless, with no results except to leave you frustrated.

Conflict doesn't just go away, though. No matter how much you may want to believe it, no one just "gets over" conflicts. This myth can lead you to the false belief that everything is okay between you two when, in fact, trouble is just burrowing in. Until the issue is resolved, it's only a heartbeat away from popping up again.

Arguments Don't Just Go Away

Arguments that *seem* to just go away are like an infection for which you take only half the antibiotics prescribed. They become the "superbugs" of arguments, reappearing later, only bigger and badder.

Don't Keep Secrets

Have you been hiding your traffic tickets or your addiction to expensive shoes, hoping that by avoiding it, you'll never have to deal with it? Not true. One of the biggest dangers in this argument pattern is that, when your mate finds out what you've been so carefully hiding (and he *will* find out), he'll feel very betrayed. Whether or not he's discovered any of your misdeeds, you need to come clean with the whole truth. If you've overspent on shoes before and he blew up, leading you to hide your illicit purchases, you need to fess up. Secrets poison a relationship. Once lies are discovered in one area, mates start to wonder *what else* you're lying about.

Gopher arguments inevitably pop up again and again, and they're usually worse each time. Your spouse will feel more and more suspicious and emotionally unsafe if you're continually hiding important information from him. Plus, you're then anxious all the time, fearful that he'll find you out. But think about how you'd feel if the tables were turned. Would you be understanding about his having some large, secret debt? Because of the mistrust they create, these kinds of secrets can be on a par with discovering an infidelity.

How to Respond to Gopher Arguments

The key to overcoming this argument tendency is to understand that the conflict will never really go away until the two of you sit down and work out the issues to reach a satisfactory result for both parties. You need to keep talking and listen hard to him if you want this "gopher" to really go away. Trying to "lay low" and keep secrets will only create mistrust and lead you in the opposite direction from where you want your relationship to go.

Arguments That Simmer

If you've been in your relationship for a long time, you've probably encountered this argument pattern. When mates struggle to know how to understand one another's "problem" with a given situation, the conflict can linger and sap your relationship strength. You both know that this thing isn't settled, but neither of you knows exactly how to settle it. It's easy in this situation to simply let the conflict simmer. It doesn't seem big enough to split up over, but it just sits quietly, making you mad or sad when you think about it.

How to Respond to Arguments That Simmer

Any significant conflict between the two of you requires understanding before you can settle it. Find out how he feels about the issue.

Ask him and then listen really hard. Do your best not to interrupt or defend yourself while he's talking. Doing those things will only shut him down or escalate the argument into a full-blown fight. Neither leads to resolution. Repeat his words so you'll be sure you understand what he said and he *knows* that you understand what he said.

Too Scary to Discuss?

Simmering arguments may seem irresolvable or too scary to even bring up. Not talking about the big issues, though, just creates even bigger problems down the line. It's difficult, but be brave. You can do it. Waiting isn't going to make it any easier.

You probably have a very different take on the issue than he does, but do you know why? You need to be able to tell him how you feel, too. Remember, when you talk about your feelings, don't say, "I feel like you want . . . ." This is just you talking about him, assuming you know what he feels, and projecting your fears on him. When you talk about your emotions, use "feeling words"—hurt, sad, angry, bitter, misunderstood, jealous, and so on. These might not sound pretty, but they'll help you get to the core of the conflict.

Start Doing This

Listen to what he's saying, not what you think he means. Make sure you're hearing what he's trying to convey by repeating his words back to him. You don't have to agree with him (you probably won't!), but you need to hear what he's saying.

Tag-Team Arguments

If you've ever watched wrestling, you know how this conflict unfolds. Tag-team arguments develop when one or more people jump into the ring during a couple's disagreement. Sometimes this happens when everyone is lubricated with alcohol. Other times, people think they need to step in to straighten you guys out.

No matter what side you're on, this can be a complicated mess. If you feel your mate isn't listening to your feelings about a situation, you might actually welcome your best friend telling your husband what she thinks is going on and how he needs to behave. But what good does that do you in the long term? How does her involvement make your partner feel? Too often, getting a third party involved results in one of you feeling ambushed. If his mom starts talking about how you "should" handle him and what you're doing wrong in your marriage, you'll probably feel upset and offended. Even though he's the one talking to his mother about your fights, you'll resent her interference and probably want to tell her that her opinions on these arguments aren't really important or helpful.

The fundamental problem with tag-team arguments is that in relationshipland, the only team that counts is that of you and your partner. No one else gets a vote, no matter how much they love you and how strong the opinions they have. It may be fun to watch in wrestling—and even seem like a good idea when you're over-whelmed with an argument—but bringing others into a relation-ship conflict ends up with someone feeling ganged up on.

How to Respond to Tag-Team Arguments

If either one of you brings another person into the argument, consider these questions in order to get a better idea of why this might be happening:

1. Do you pull others into your fights to try to make or reinforce a point?
2. Is this tag-team fighting happening because one or both of you feels that your partner won't hear you unless you get someone else's *support* to prove a point? If so, practice the listen-and-

repeat techniques described earlier in this chapter before you get to the point of having public fights, and certainly before either of you feels the need to pull in a third party. If you two can really hear each other, you shouldn't need anyone else to say it a different way.

3. Do you have to drink before you talk about the problems? If so, you're clouding your judgment, impairing your ability to listen, and risking your safety. Alcohol and drugs only fuel arguments; they do not solve them.

4. Is one of you afraid to talk to the other alone? If this is true because you are afraid you might be physically hurt, seek out professional help. Sometimes, however, individuals just feel overwhelmed by the other person and think they're not going to be listened to if they speak themselves. If this is the case, getting help from a therapist gives you a buffer.

Your answers to these questions should help pinpoint the reason the tag-teaming is happening. Solving the root problem behind why you're tag-teaming will greatly increase your ability to solve the argument itself.

Public Arguments

You've probably been at a friend's birthday party or a club when two of your friends began having—or continued having—a very public argument. They may have even tried to draft others to back them up, with their friends scattering to avoid having to take sides. Maybe you've been at the center of this scenario yourself. What starts as "kidding around" with your significant other shifts into something very real and emotional. You didn't mean to, but you end up in a full-blown argument right there in front of everyone.

This kind of situation can be embarrassing, but also liberating, because you might garner public support if you think other people see him the way *you* see him. In these scenarios, you can find

yourself replaying unresolved arguments you've had before or starting entirely new ones. You might end up in a fight over something
you've been brooding about but haven't mentioned, telling yourself
it isn't really worth starting a fight. Then, *bang*, you're fighting about
it right there in front of everyone.

Keep It Private

No matter who chooses to go public with arguments, it's pretty
much guaranteed to make someone uncomfortable. For the sake
of your friends and for your own benefit, keep your arguments
between the two of you—no audience, please. After all, you're
not getting paid to perform in a reality television show.

Or, maybe you'd like to keep things toned down in public—
something your mother said about not airing your dirty linen in
front of others—but your mate seems to think this is the perfect
time to talk about all the things that are bothering him. He might
try this tactic if he thinks you aren't listening to him in private. You
may try to send him a "let's talk about this *later*" look. Or you may
try to laugh it off, but if he continues enlisting friends to back him
up, you'll feel you have to defend yourself. This can be a very difficult situation for everyone and doesn't yield any positive results.

Then there are the silent arguments that are carried on in public.
In this scenario, you can cut the tension between you with a knife
even when you're with your friends. Don't kid yourself. If you're in
the middle of a massive argument with your mate, your friends will
be able to sense this. Silent arguments involve others just by their
being in the same space.

How to Respond to Public Arguments

Deal with issues in private, just between the two of you, *before*
heading into a public situation. If you don't have the time to finish

the discussion before you have to be somewhere, make an agreement to table it until you're alone again.

Attack/Apologize

This is a style of argument that involves one—or both—of you angrily venting. In this kind of fight, you find yourself getting really, really angry and you let yourself go. You say just what you've been thinking and you don't mince words. Maybe you've been mad about this kind of situation before; maybe you've been at this place in a relationship before (maybe even in *this* relationship). Let's say you've been cheated on or lied to or misunderstood one time too many, and you blow up. You call your partner names, accuse him of unspeakable crimes, and tell him you know he doesn't love you. He loves his mother (or his dog or his BlackBerry) more than you. You're hurt, you're pissed, and you need to tell him just how upset you feel. Venting seems natural now, and you need to let it all out.

> ### Don't Try to Even the Score
> When you love someone, he has the ability to make you mad or hurt you more than anyone else. This makes you vulnerable. Feeling vulnerable can make you want to hurt him as badly as he's hurt you. But in the end, all you've done is add to the hurt in the relationship rather than solve the issue at hand.

Then, you feel better. You've blown off some steam. You're able to calm down some. As far as you're concerned, that was a cleansing venting session. Your partner, however, may be sitting in stunned silence, feeling like he's just been gunned down. Every word you've said has been like a nail and you've hammered this pretty hard. You feel better because you've let loose, but he doesn't. Suddenly you realize you got carried away. Now that you've calmed down, you even apologize for some of the things you said.

However, even though you apologize, your mate can't seem to get past what you said. You're not mad anymore, but now he's angry. You may not understand why he can't move beyond the misunderstanding. He doesn't understand how you can be so angry and then act like it didn't happen. You're at a stalemate.

How to Respond to the Attack/Apologize Style

Attacking the one you love never helps, even if you're very, very hurt and angry. Remember that even though you don't feel loving now, you do love your partner. You can learn to express yourselves so the other person understands, but this will mean adjustments on both parts.

Talk when he's not in the middle of something else or when you're not raging mad. Sometimes taking a deep breath or chilling for a while will give you a better frame of reference for a productive discussion. You need to listen to him when he's *ready* to talk, not necessarily when you *want* him to talk. He needs to hear your concerns and feelings, too.

This won't happen if you attempt to communicate by telling him what he's done (right or wrong) or should do. Real, true communication doesn't happen until you talk productively about your emotions and hear his feelings, even if these aren't spoken in exactly the same way you would say it.

When Your Partner Thinks You're the "Problem"

Now that you've identified one or more argument patterns, it may seem that your partner thinks the transgressor—the one who screws up—is always you. He has probably said that he's tried to fix the problems. You're the screwup, the one who can't quite do things right, the one who doesn't care about the relationship. It can be difficult to sort out who's at fault or who's to blame for the problems in the relationship, but you need to assume that you both have responsibility for at least half the problem.

> ### It Takes Two
> It takes two people to create conflict in a relationship. Never think it's all your fault or all his fault. Neither one of you is that all-powerful.

He may be very, very convinced that he's done everything he could do. He's tried to fix it and it might seem to him like you're not trying at all. To some extent, you might actually agree with him, either because you want to believe you have the power to fix the problems in the relationship (though you don't, since you're only one-half of it) or because you're accustomed to assuming that whatever is wrong must be because of you (because he has repeatedly told you this).

You might keep making mistakes—particularly doing things he's asked you not to do—even though you're really trying to improve. These mistakes are part of being human, but they're also frustrating. You might hear from him about mistakes you never knew were mistakes. If you're very emotional, he might see you as trying to manipulate him through your feelings. If you internalize to the point of showing no feelings, he might accuse you of just not caring. Sometimes, you probably get mad enough not to care. In any case, he's trying to instill in you the belief that you're the problem with the relationship. That can never be the case, however. Each person is 50 percent responsible for the health of the relationship.

 Say This to Him
"We're both important in this relationship and, if we're going to fix it, we both need to look at our issues. I'm looking at mine."

Even if you've made mistakes, you're not completely at fault. He may be able to list all the ways he's tried to make this work over and over, but that doesn't make you more at fault than you already are.

Where Do You Fit In?

After reviewing the styles presented in this chapter, think about the following questions.

1. Look at your typical argument pattern and ask yourself what your role in it is. Be honest with yourself, but not condemning. You aren't doing this to punish yourself; you're simply trying to learn from past unproductive behavior.

2. Think about what your argument style gets you. No matter which style is yours, you use it because it brings you some reward. Try not to be critical of yourself. For example, you might use the sniper fire pattern out of anger and hurt and in an attempt to avoid relationship repercussions that seem to come with an open discussion of your feelings (if you even recognize these). Maybe you use the attack/apologize method because your partner eventually accepts your apology and lets you "win." Keep in mind, though, that the "reward" isn't really about winning in the everyday sense. In relationship conflict, "winning" is about feeling understood and valued for who you are. Knowing what your reward will be can help you understand why you argue the way you do and can help you change your behavior if necessary.

Recognize Your Positive Steps

Ask yourself if you've identified your unproductive argument patterns and tried to make them more productive through the techniques given in this chapter. Having some or all of these conflict patterns doesn't mean that you should get out of the relationship, nor does it mean that you should stay in. It just means that now you see what you need to work on. You two have made progress if you have:

- Identified how you argue (which can help you assess the relationship more objectively).
- Tried to productively address the conflict—between the two of you—rather than avoid it.
- Truly listened to one another, even if you don't initially understand or disagree. Listen harder. This can be very difficult, but it's an essential skill to learn.

Give yourself credit for taking a really serious look at the relationship and attempting to find out what's not working. This kind of self-reflection is really difficult, but it's the only way to see what needs to be changed. You should be proud of your strength of character and of your resolve to improve the way you two communicate.

- **You should stay if:** You're both willing to use more effective communication. You are willing to work to recognize your part in the argument pattern and to make changes.
- **You should leave if:** Your fights leave you feeling battered and violated.

Exercises and Affirmations

Now that you know some of the common argument types, it's time to take a good look at your own. Take a deep breath and think about your strong points. You are in the middle of a difficult decision. It's easy to forget that you have many good characteristics. Write down one of your good qualities and put it where you'll see it every day. You don't have to post it in a public place if you don't want to, but you need to remind yourself how you benefit others.

chapter four

The Five Biggest Relationship Conflicts

Things to Consider

- Are both of you willing to eventually negotiate on problem areas?
- Have you really talked—without recrimination—about what bothers you the most?
- Do the two of you want very different lives? *You can be very different from your mate and still want the same things.*

Now that you've determined how you and your partner fight and have learned how you can argue more productively, let's take a look at the most common subjects couples fight about. As you think about your specific conflicts within these common subjects, remember the listen-and-repeat technique (explained in Chapter 3) and other healthy lines of communication. You may find that your arguments on these subjects fall in the "Arguments That Simmer" category because they are so important that they'll keep coming up until they are resolved.

Quiz: What Issues Are Central to Your Conflicts?

On a scale of one to five (with one meaning you disagree strongly and five meaning you agree strongly), answer the following questions:

1. You have an unsatisfactory sex life. _____
2. You argue over everything about raising your kids (or whether or not to have kids). _____
3. Your money conflicts are driving you apart. _____
4. You don't agree on your religious beliefs—or the lack thereof. _____
5. You can't agree on spending time with your families. _____

If you scored 20–25 points: You two disagree about most or all key issues; it's amazing that you've made it this far in your relationship.

If you scored 11–19 points: You two aren't on the same page about some main issues but do agree on others. To be happy with your mate, you need to find a way to resolve those significant areas of disagreement.

If you scored 5–10 points: While they can be distressing, your conflicts are not widespread or pervasive.

Couple conflicts tend to fall into specific areas. Even if you don't have conflicts within the "big five" as discussed in this chapter, you still have to address problems, no matter where they arise. If you scored in the 5–10 point range on this quiz yet still feel very disconnected from your partner, return to your list of criteria from Chapter 2 and use that as your "quiz." Knowing the specific area from which your arguments stem can help you decide if you want to work them out.

Relationship Conflict #1: Money

Money is the number one area of conflict in relationships. Just think of all the components: How it's spent, who's spending it, who makes how much, how much is saved. More couples report splitting up over this issue than any other.

Approaching Money in Different Ways

People generally fall into two different camps when it comes to money—those who save, and those who spend:

- **Savers** are concerned about their retirement accounts, the kids' college educations, and late fees, and generally are allergic to having a balance on their credit cards.
- **Spenders** don't see the point in getting all bent out of shape about using some of a savings account. After all, the money is there; why not use it?

The problem arises, of course, if one of you is a saver and the other is a spender. This common scenario can lead to all sorts of conflicts, big and small. Because money conflicts reach right down into the core of a person, these arguments often touch on fears about security and issues such as personal freedom. Do you keep joint accounts? Do you have a right to insist your partner spend—or save—money the way you do? These differences can bring a relationship down, even if you love one another.

Understand Where Your Partner Is Coming From

Even if your partner's feelings are very different from yours, it's important that you understand where he's coming from. The differences in the way you handled money might even have been attractive when you first met (perhaps you liked that he spent a lot of money to take you on nice vacations), but the same thing you liked about him then may now be the source of some of your conflict (perhaps you think he spends too freely). In order to jump-start a conversation that will uncover your basic attitudes toward money, start by asking each other the following questions:

- How did your family deal with money when you were growing up?
- What, if anything, worries you about our financial situation?
- How would you like to change our spending habits? Our saving habits?
- How do you feel when you spend money? Does it make you feel great or does it scare you?

In the beginning of your relationship, the way you two handled money may have seemed like no big deal. You probably never saw a difference in financial styles as a reason to end the relationship. Yet money means freedom, power, and a reward to most people—concepts that can elicit strong feelings if your partner doesn't feel the same way you do. When you marry a person, you may even marry your credit history with that person's (depending on where you live), and few things are more personal than credit histories.

The Problem with Separate Accounts
Some couples attempt to avoid money conflicts by not sharing income—they split everything, including living expenses, child care costs, and vacation costs. If you're legally married, though, your credit may be affected by what he does, and vice versa (depending on where you live and your specific situation; contact a lawyer for more information).

Keeping separate accounts is sidestepping the issue, at best. Now that women are earning their own livelihoods and sometimes making more money than do men, the independence that comes with keeping your money separated can sound healthy. Ask yourself why you're maintaining separate accounts. (Are you hiding your bank statements from the guy you walk around naked in front of?) If the reason is that you have different approaches to money, you're just *avoiding* the problem. Your differences will eventually come up again. Let's say you are a spender, your husband is a saver, and you two decide to stay together but keep separate accounts. What will you do if you run out of money during your retirement? Will he help fund your retirement? If, on the other hand, you decide to separate and he has run up lots of debt, you may be still responsible for paying it off even if you maintained separate accounts during your marriage.

Financial Infidelity

How you handle money may be hiding other issues. Some people feel that their partner is engaging in "financial cheating"—spending money without talking about it first, or even keeping his or her spending a secret. If this is the case in your relationship (whether you are the one "cheating" or being "cheated on"), you need to deal with this issue. Getting professional help is a good option, but at the least, you need to explore what money represents to both the cheater and the cheated. Money means different things to different people. Getting to the core problem will go a long way toward helping you resolve money issues.

A Solution

The key to overcoming money conflicts is to find a way to accommodate both your concerns. For example, to help make the saver feel comfortable with a luxury vacation, the spender may have to put away money several months in advance. And to show the saver that he understands her concerns, the spender may have to find a way to enjoy buying to a scaled-back degree—for example, choosing the 48-inch TV instead of the 60-inch. There has to be room in your relationship for what each of you wants so that both of you can accept certain saving/splurging boundaries.

Relationship Conflict #2: Sex

Sexual intimacy is an area of a relationship that begins in an exciting, happy way with the flush of new love but sometimes deteriorates as a couple grows together. At first, you probably rushed to rip off each other's clothes. But now, you two may fight about any number of issues, including how often you get it, how good it is, and even who you're doing it with!

If you two have lingering disagreements about *anything* in your relationship, chances are good that your sex life will be affected. This area of a relationship is like the canary in the coal mine. When the sex life dies or goes on life support, you need to pay attention. Problems in this area can reflect more than simply what's going on in the bedroom. There's nothing "just" about sex. Unless one or both of you have had untreated sexual trauma, your sexual experience is actually a sign of the overall health of your relationship.

Common Sexual Problems

When one partner feels she's constantly asking the other for sex—or vice versa—there are problems lurking, and not just under the covers. Here are just a few common situations you and your partner may be facing:

- **One of us is not getting enough.** Before you chalk it up to having very different sex drives, look at communication and power issues between you two. Some people shut off the tap, so to speak, when they're not happy with some aspect of the relationship (and it's *not* just women who do this!).

- **One (or both) of you isn't having fun.** If one or the other of you isn't enjoying the sex, but just "goes along," the relationship will most likely break down eventually. Sex is a mutual experience, and it should take both partners' needs into account.
- **One of you wants more kinky sex.** People tend to get coy about this subject, but the level of variety and variation in your sex life needs to be something the two of you agree on. Both have to find it fulfilling. Too often, one or the other just goes along.
- **One partner has been unfaithful.** This is one of the most painful, confusing experiences a couple can address. No one steps out when the current relationship is fulfilling. If the two of you are open and honest with one another—and you're happy and secure in the relationship and with your sex life—there's no need to be looking for companionship elsewhere. When a partner goes outside a relationship, there's a problem *in* the relationship.

The Grass Isn't Always Greener

Few people intend to cheat on their partners. Extracurricular relationships tend to feel magical and different, but in the end, they aren't. It may feel like love, but if there have been problems—spoken or not—in the primary relationship, they can show up in any other. The underlying issues need to be addressed rather than one of you just moving on to another relationship.

Infidelity

If a relationship suffers from infidelity, the couple faces a long, rocky road to reconnection. The wronged person typically expects the cheater to grovel and beg to remain, but that won't help long-term. What will actually heal the relationship is to see the problems that existed *before* the cheating. To the betrayed partner, this fact can feel like she or he is being blamed for the affair, but that's not the case. Cheating is a choice only the cheater made. The betrayed spouse is in no way to blame. However, that doesn't mean there wasn't trouble in the relationship beforehand.

Relationships are a lot like plumbing. Everything works great as long as the main line (your emotions) doesn't get clogged.

Rebecca's Story:

Adam and I were college sweethearts and we've been married five years. He is an architect and he got a job right out of college with a good firm. I joined a large company's public relations department. We can afford to drive nice cars and we sometimes hang out with friends. We talked about having kids in a few years.

But, I have to admit I'm getting tired of Adam's increasing isolation. He's been avoiding going out for some time and the fights that popped up in our college years have started reappearing. We have begun having spats over housework and vacations. Pretty much all we do is work and fight. I'm starting to feeling old, like I left my youth behind. Adam seems to think I shouldn't want to have fun with friends any longer, so he just stays home and I go out. But I'm tired of doing everything by myself. Adam never seems interested in talking and he never acts like he cares about what's going on in my job.

Our sex life has really suffered. I know he's looking at porn and, while this really bothered me at first, lately I really don't care. I guess sometimes I'm relieved not to have to deal with him. Over the last few months, I've been growing closer to a guy at work. Jeremy's fun and he thinks I'm funny, too. He likes talking to me and he's said how smart he thinks I am. Our friendship just grew from there. His marriage isn't very fulfilling, either, so we had a lot of experiences in common. Eventually, I was texting him from home in the evenings and he kept me up on what was (or wasn't) going on with him. Before we realized it, we started having feelings for one another. One day after a work lunch, he kissed me and, while I've never thought I'd ever have an affair, I found myself falling for him. I feel giddy when we talk and depressed when I can't see him. Everything with Adam is so hard, but it's different with Jeremy. Everything seems so natural and easy.

Few people intend to get into affairs, often saying things like "it just happened." If a person is unhappy in her primary relationship, she might seek connection elsewhere. Even if this affair is of the nonsexual, emotional variety, there still is a gripping intimacy. It's all fun—after all, you don't have to deal with day-to-day issues (bills, kids, social activities) in an affair. If it develops into a "real" relationship, you will soon have to deal with those things all over again. Yet starting a relationship in secrecy doesn't lend itself to healthy relationship development.

Porn and Emotional Distance

Some people feel safer baring their bodies than their souls. The use of and addiction to porn is a growing problem and an indication of the difficulties couples are having with emotional intimacy. Porn gives the illusion of contact with others without the complications and challenges of relationships.

If she's going to be happy in this marriage, Rebecca needs to tell Adam how she feels about him not socializing. She needs to encourage him to develop friendships in his area of interest and to insist on his going out with her as well. In order to indicate that she sees his side of things, she needs to keep their social interactions short and not expect him to be the extrovert she is. If he wants to save their relationship, Adam is going to have to adjust his behavior to some of Rebecca's needs. Indulging excessively in pornography is a sign that Adam's emotional intimacy needs aren't met. If the two of them deal with their issues in a way that makes them both feel important and powerful, outside sexual stimuli won't have the pull for him that they do now. In addition to crafting a social life they both can live with, he needs to turn off the porn and start talking to Rebecca—about the conflicts as well as his desire to be with her.

Relationship Conflict #3: Kids

One of the biggest misconceptions about relationships is that having children will automatically bring you and your partner closer together. On the contrary, the first area of conflict for some couples is whether or not to have children. Even if you agree on the decision to have children, you still face a plethora of topics you may disagree on later—parenting styles, discipline, having enough money for college educations, child care, and so on. The best time to talk about kids is before you have them, so you have a clear understanding about your attitudes and feelings regarding parenthood. That's the way it should work, but few think to do it this way.

Get on the Same Page *Before* You Have Kids

You two may have entered parenthood assuming you were going to agree about everything. When it comes to parenthood, couples get lost in the fun stuff (as with weddings) of getting gifts and picking out names. These are only the superficial issues, though—there's certainly much more to parenthood than which stroller you pick out. You both bring your own experiences as children. You probably know the kind of parent you *don't* want to be, and you may both have images of how to be a good parent. But those may be vague ideas, and you need to think in concrete terms. Have you talked in detail about the kind of parents you want to be? Are you in agreement about the kind of love and discipline you want to show your kids? These questions are important to answer in order to present a united front to your children, and to help them feel safe and secure. If you already have children but hadn't discussed these issues yet, it's never too late to start!

Bridget's Story:

When Carter and I got married, I tried not to get too crazy about the wedding. We'd been together four years and marriage seemed like a natural extension. When we'd been married for two years, Carter finished school. We then were both earning decent money. Having kids was something we always both wanted, and it seemed like the time. All our friends were having children.

But after our son was born, everything got complicated. Carter's always been a social guy, going out with his friends. I thought he would scale that back now that we have a son. He goes out just as much, though, and stays longer hours at work. I know he's trying to be a good employee and make a decent living for our family, but he's still spending a lot of time with his guy friends. I end up feeling stuck at home with our baby. When I mention this, Carter just says he has to stay longer at work and he feels like he deserves some time to be with the guys. He says he doesn't see why I'm freaking out. When I suggested he spend more time at home with us, rather than hanging out with his friends every weekend, he just picked up the baby and his bag and said I should go off and chill, he'd take care of the boy. But I want the *three* of us to spend time together!

I know I probably sound like a control freak, but Carter can't just take our son with him whenever he wants to hang out with the guys. Gavin needs some structure in his life! He needs to be home with his dad, not to be hauled around. Carter just needs to do less socializing. I think he should adjust to my needs and our son's needs and stay home sometimes.

I know Carter feels like I'm telling him what to do all the time. He says since he's taking care of the baby and I have time to myself, he doesn't see what I'm complaining about. We argue all the time and he says he feels nagged, but I keep trying to tell him he's always blowing me off.

We both love our son, but we can't seem to find one another anymore.

For Bridget and Carter to make this relationship work, they need to sit down and talk about the fears that came with parenthood. Even though she's not feeling that Carter cares for and values her, Bridget needs to really listen to him, without making judgmental comments or pointing out his flaws as a father. If these two are going to make it as a couple, Carter has to realize he's important to his wife and new son and see that they need and want his presence. Bridget wants to control everything parental in her desire to do everything *right*, but she needs to loosen up and let Carter find his own parenting style. He's got to have room to be his own valuable, significant, unique person with his son.

Determine Your Parenting Styles

When you have a baby, you enjoy a lot of powerful, fulfilling experiences. You also have a lot of decisions to make. Should the baby sleep in your bed or in a crib? Schedule or no schedule? And that's only the first few months. If you and your partner disagree about some aspect of parenting, it's time to take a step back and evaluate the situation as objectively as you can. Start by answering the following questions.

ASK YOURSELF:
1. Do my partner and I parent *together*?
2. Do I think that he ought to feel the same about parenting as I do?
3. Am I staying in this relationship only because I don't want my child to have divorced parents?
4. Is our being together making our child's life better or worse?

Try to step outside your own natural desire to be a "good" parent, and be as truthful with yourself as you can. Being honest with yourself will enable you to give your child the best. Your answers to these questions will help you reach your decision on whether to stay or go.

Discipline

This is a major area of conflict for some families. If one of you believes in the value of judicious spanking and the other is adamantly opposed to striking the child, you're definitely not on the same page. You can't hide this kind of disagreement from your children, so you need to talk about your feelings and decide on a mutually agreeable discipline strategy. The two of you probably have your own strengths and weaknesses; determine what they are and use them to your child's best interest.

Favoritism

Unless you were an only child, you have probably dealt with favoritism at some level yourself. Most people with siblings—whether they were the "favorite" or not—can say which parent preferred which child. If this is the case with you or your mate, you'll be particularly sensitive to him seeming to prefer one child over the other. Sharing your feelings about your own childhood may help him see the possible effect of his actions. If you talk about this without attacking him, he might be able to see your concerns.

Child Care

Men today are more involved in the actual care of their children—certainly more than their fathers—but women still bear a significantly larger part. This gap tends to show up in the middle of arguments, with men wanting to feel acknowledged for their involvement. Some women feel that they have to pat their partners on the back for every dance class the father takes his kids to.

Say This to Him

"I'm sure I haven't always been fair to you, but I really do want what is best for us both."

Women still do the majority of the laundry, housecleaning, and shopping, though—along with the majority of the child care. This imbalance of responsibilities can cause a lot of resentment if you both have careers and limited time. Talk about how to handle chores, so each person has some responsibility and each has some personal time. Arrange a schedule that works for both partners. Break down the chores involved in parenting and do your best to dispassionately discuss these. Be realistic about the career demands you both face, but don't accept that you—as the mother—should automatically do more. Redistributing the child care will give you both more opportunity to enjoy your children.

Relationship Conflict #4: Family

Relationships with family members (your own and his) can be complicated, fiery, and difficult, just like your own as a married couple. Not liking his family brings obvious conflicts—unless he doesn't like them either. Yet even if he dislikes his family, he may feel he has to respect them and see them on holidays or at reunions. He might even say you don't understand his relatives if you say something disparaging about them (even if he's said the same disparaging thing before!).

Navigate family relationships carefully. You should both work out issues with your own families—in your own time and your own way. Then each of you needs to do the same with your partner's family, establishing relationships with them without putting your spouse in the middle.

If a member of his family really dislikes you, you might find yourself arguing with your partner about this person. The closer the relationship he has with the individual who doesn't like you, the more this can become an issue between the two of you. While you don't have to love his relatives, you do need to understand that he loves them. Family is important to most people and, while relationship boundaries and personal information need to be respected, it's important to come to see the value of family relationships, even if it's not your family.

Family connections complicate an already complicated situation. You might find that you love his family. This is usually great—unless you find you're not sure you love him anymore. Some people hesitate to leave unhappy relationships because they don't want to lose their husband's family. Even if this feels like a compelling reason, you shouldn't stay simply for your in-laws. The health of the primary relationship between you and your partner is infinitely more important.

Relationship Conflict #5: Religion

Religious beliefs run deep, but conflict about religion within a relationship can initially seem either insignificant or easy to solve when it may not be either. Some couples who grow up in different faiths have a hard time seeing one another's views. When one of you feels strongly either for or against religion, this belief has the potential to be a flashpoint in the relationship. Strain also results from widely differing perspectives about the role religion should play in your lives.

If you and your partner didn't discuss this type of religious difference early on in your relationship, start now. Hear each other out; listen carefully and with respect. Determine if there is a middle ground that can make both parties happy and fulfilled spiritually. If the issue is where you attend church, you can take turns attending each others' services. You both deserve to have your spiritual views respected.

Bonus Conflict #6: Housework (It's True!)

The previous five areas may give the two of you a hard time, but you would expect them to be big deals—money, sex, kids, family, and religion are very important! The division of housework, however, is a major area of conflict for many couples and yet they typically feel that it shouldn't be "as big a deal" as it is. Well, it *is* a big deal.

Decades ago, no one argued about housework because women were responsible for child care and housework and men brought home the paycheck. Now that women work outside the home (some even work longer hours and make more money than their mates!), the housework issue has been turned on its head. That's how a lot of couples end up screaming over who empties the dishwasher.

How the house is kept (or not kept) is a daily reflection of the communication between the two of you. If you both enjoy polishing the countertops, you probably don't fight about this topic. More likely, however, you disagree about how much should be done, who should do it, and when. Think about how you have decided who did what thus far in your relationship. Whether you realize it or not, you have both brought preconceived ideas about housework into the relationship. If, like most couples, you haven't examined these ideas before conflict breaks out, do so now.

Every couple will need to determine what arrangement works for them. But remember that the relationship is more important than a little dust on a shelf. Keep things in perspective and do what works for both of you. Remember that you don't have the right to insist that your partner change his cleanliness comfort level to match yours. You simply need to be able to compromise on a cleanliness level that enables your household to run smoothly.

Recognize Your Positive Steps

The conflicts discussed in this chapter are indeed the most common, but they're also the most difficult to resolve. The topics may evoke passionate feelings, childhood memories, expectations of each gender, and fears of the future—all of which are challenging to talk about constructively and objectively. Most relationship problems in this area won't be fixed in one conversation; you and your partner will need to continue working on them for a long time. However, celebrate any small victories you achieve along the way. It's important to reward yourselves for your hard work.

You and your partner are making progress if you:

- Truly listened, without prejudgment, to your partner's views on a subject
- Shared your feelings honestly and without blame
- Discovered why you have fundamentally different opinions about a certain topic
- Began to see a compromise on the horizon

Recognizing your progress helps you and your partner see that problems *can* be fixed if you work hard enough. If you and your partner do *not* see any progress, however—if you repeat the same complaints, refuse to compromise, and resort to yelling—these problems may be too significant to overcome.

- **You should stay if:** You only have conflict in one or two areas and you can talk logically, without a lot of emotion, about these.
- **You should leave if:** You have conflicts in four out of the five areas (or all five) and you can't resolve any of these with the techniques suggested in this book.

Exercises and Affirmations

Spend some time in personal reflection. Make sure you know what you need to feel fulfilled in any areas where you and your partner currently have conflicts. Make a list of these needs—either written or mental. Stay true to them as you discuss problems with your partner.

As you think about what you want out of life, pay attention to your own thoughts about yourself. You may be saying very negative things about your behavior—things probably not valid if you spoke from an objective, nonemotional perspective. You may be dwelling on inaccurate, hurtful beliefs about yourself. When you catch yourself thinking these thoughts, grab the reins and turn your thoughts in another direction. Refuse to keep repeating ugly self-talk.

chapter five

Determine the Real Reason You're in This Relationship

Things to Consider

- Why did this relationship work for you in the beginning?
- Do the reasons you got into this relationship still exist?
- Were these healthy reasons that can help you grow as a person?
- Are there new reasons to stay?

There's nothing simple about considering ending a committed relationship. If it wasn't good—at some point—you probably wouldn't even still be in it. Knowing why you're still here now is an important factor to consider when you assess whether you need to stay or leave. I always ask my clients, "Why are you here instead of in a lawyer's office?" It helps them to focus on why they haven't left yet. The reasons you got into this relationship might still be there, or they may have disappeared or changed.

In this chapter, we'll look at some of the most common reasons people stay in a relationship:

- You have shared friends and you don't want to give up the larger community of people who are important to you.

- You have a shared lifestyle and you like living in the place you live, vacationing at the places you vacation, and driving the cars you drive. You like having a husband who fits into the life you want.
- You have children together and you worry that leaving will really, really distress them, and possibly stunt your children forever.
- You're trying to prove something. If you've come from a family in which no one divorces, being the first to divorce can be difficult. On the other hand, your family may be littered with exes and you want to be different.
- He's a "safe" guy. With him, you don't worry about being cheated on or left.
- You fear you have no other options for a better partner. Lots of people wonder if there is no one else out there for them.
- You don't have enough motivation to leave. Leaving takes a lot of effort. Maybe you're settling because you've gotten comfortable with being uncomfortable.
- You're afraid of the dating scene.
- You're simply afraid.
- You're staying out of habit.

Though all of these reasons are emotional, compelling, and powerful, none of them alone is a valid reason to stay in a relationship.

Quiz: Why Are You Still in the Relationship?

On a scale of one to five (with one meaning you disagree strongly and five meaning you agree strongly), answer the following questions:

1. You stay because you don't want to lose the other things (house, family, income) that would go along with him. _____
2. Sometimes you think you might be confusing concern for him with love. _____

3. You stay because you want to conquer whatever challenges he presents. _____

4. You're only staying because you don't want to hurt him. _____

5. You're already emotionally involved with someone else. _____

If you scored 20 or more points: You're staying in the relationship for unhealthy reasons (such as guilt, fear, or power), not because you still love him.

If you scored 11–19 points: Some of the reasons you're staying are healthy; others are not.

If you scored 5–10 points: The relationship has hit some speed bumps, but is probably worth working out.

You Have Shared Friends and a Shared Community

Did the two of you meet in high school (or junior high) and your best friend was dating his best friend? Adolescence is an anxious time—everyone is unsure and trying to prove to others, and to themselves, that they can handle all the important aspects of adulthood . . . including romantic relationships. You may have been dating around, flirting with whomever crossed your path. When the one who would become your partner happened to be in your path, you were probably excited to find that someone of the opposite sex was interested in you. Even if the two of you didn't get together until you were out of adolescence, the power of having shared friends can be significant.

Getting together with someone who's part of your group of friends is very natural and can seem like a good idea. *Staying* with someone because of shared friendships can be more complicated, however. Even if *your* best friend is married to *his* best friend, the two of you still need to have an intimate connection all your own.

How Your Shared Friends Might Affect Your Decision

Leaving a relationship in which you've enjoyed a strong community of friends can feel like you have to leave your whole life. This is scary! Do you find yourself wondering who gets which friends, and how this is going to work if you split? Will your friends hang out with you or with him? Will you have to choose who goes to which events so you won't bump into each other?

This factor isn't as trivial as it may sound. Friendship is massively important—it prolongs your life and makes you stronger. In a 1992 longevity study of people aged seventy and older, researchers in Australia concluded that a network of good friends is more likely even than close family relationships to increase longevity in older people. As you decide whether to stay or go, you might find yourself feeling pressured by friends, one way or the other. For example, if your best girlfriend has been divorced for a while, she might not understand why you're staying and working on the relationship. After all, she took the step and probably feels she's doing pretty well. And, too, you've probably complained about him to her often.

On the other hand, having had a shared community might strengthen your sense that you should stay with him. After all, these people are important to you. You can't take the relationship out of that context, so if you leave him, you might have to leave all of them as well. Even though you might have found one another through these friends, your relationship with your partner needs to stand on its own.

The Bottom Line: You Need to Think of Yourself First

Your friends and family care about both of you. They're involved in this relationship and in whether you stay or go, to some degree. However, you can't make your decision solely on how other people in your life will be affected. You have to put your own feelings and needs first.

If you've developed close relationships with his friends and family, you might hate the thought of not being at their picnics or holiday celebrations. Maybe you don't want to "divorce" them too. Suddenly your decision of whether to stay or go isn't just about the two of you—it's about all of these other people with whom you share your life. But remember that *you're* the one who has to live in this relationship every minute of every day, not just on special occasions when everyone's having fun. If your relationship with these people is strong enough, it will continue even if you choose to leave. If it's not, then you will have an opportunity to make new, stronger friendships.

You Have a Shared Lifestyle

If you and your partner share a number of the following items in common, you probably have a shared lifestyle:

- Hobbies/activities
- Hangouts

- Habits (good or bad)
- Background—social or economic
- Profession
- Religious beliefs
- Ethnicity
- Life goals

Most couples *do* share a number of items on this list. Some of these shared interests or values likely brought you two together in the first place. If your relationship begins to falter, however, these shared lifestyle connections can make your decision to stay or go more complicated.

How a Shared Lifestyle Can Bring a Couple Together

Work is a natural place for singles to meet other singles and relationships to develop. If you and your partner work in the same field, you may find that you're able to talk to him about things occurring in your day that you can't really share with your friends or family. This very easy connection can strengthen the relationship.

Drinking as a Social Connection
Simply hanging out at the same bar can create a mutuality of lifestyle. Having drinks at the same place with the same people every Friday night may not seem to constitute a major connection, but it does. If excessive drinking or recreational drugs are a significant part of your life, however, these behaviors—which might have been part of what drew you together—are likely to also help tear you apart. Remember, alcohol and drugs only fuel problems; they don't solve them.

You also might be drawn to people who share your activities outside of work. Perhaps you went to the same church as your mate, and this pulled you together. If you have similar beliefs, your relationship may have blossomed partly due to this sense of camaraderie and understanding.

Having the same lifestyle interests, though, doesn't necessarily mean you don't have conflict. Even if you share religious beliefs and go to the same church, you might still fight about money or sex or any number of other things. Having the same lifestyle doesn't mean being conflict-free.

The Bottom Line: Think of the Big Picture

If you're thinking about staying with someone simply because of your shared lifestyle, consider a few questions. Is it possible for you to find another partner who likes the same things as you? And do your mutual interests override the conflicts in your relationship? While your shared lifestyle is an important component of your relationship, you two also need to share mutual respect and love. If you don't, no amount of cycling or chats about work will help.

You Are Trying to Prove Something

The choices you make as an adult are a culmination of everything that has happened in your life thus far. If the people you grew up with damaged your self-esteem, you may still be dealing with the long-term effects of those wounds. You may be tempted to stay in your relationship simply to prove other people wrong—people who said hurtful things such as:

- You'll never be able to get a guy.
- He's too hot for you.
- He's too good for you.

- You can't keep a guy who makes good money.
- He'll find someone better.

An act of defiance sometimes lies at the center of relationship choices. When the preacher's son marries a stripper, there's a message in the act. You might have entered into this relationship because you knew that certain people in your life would be shocked, upset, or impressed by it. This isn't to suggest that you just pretended to love him or that you never loved him; it's just that the issues you brought into adulthood have an impact on who you're with.

Did he have what you lacked? If you saw your life as financially or emotionally disadvantaged, you might have liked him even more because of his strengths in those areas. Whether you were attracted to your partner because he's good-looking and you felt unattractive or because his family has money and yours didn't, it's important to recognize these factors.

Why Do You Feel You Have Something to Prove?

Some people grow up feeling inadequate. Whether they think they're not smart enough or pretty enough or rich enough, some individuals come into a relationship looking for an emotional "patch." If you're aware of these vulnerabilities, you might think your inadequacies force you to make bad choices. If this is true, you might have a tendency to be drawn to a man who made you more "okay."

Sometimes the very traits you were initially attracted to because they provided this "patch" end up being the traits that drive you two apart. Did you grow up feeling scared and small and end up marrying someone you saw as never doubting himself? In the beginning, you probably felt grateful that you got to hook your wagon to his star. As time went on, however, you may have found it difficult to be in a relationship with a guy who's never wrong. In this scenario, you're likely to end up being *wrong* way too much of the time.

Elise's Story:

Jackson worked for my father's company, functioning in a junior capacity, when I temped there while I attended our local college. When we started dating, I knew my dad liked Jackson and thought he was a hard worker.

Jackson and I dated for a year and, when I graduated from college, he proposed. When I look back, I see that our dating life and married years revolved around my father's company and Jackson's job there. I started teaching first grade at an elementary school in our town and we bought a house close to my parents.

In two years, I got pregnant and had our first child. Jackson continued working long hours at Dad's company and we frequently socialized with my parents. After our second child was born, two years later, I started feeling depressed. I went to my OB and was treated for postpartum depression. It got better and I went back to work, but I've became aware of feeling unhappy and dissatisfied with my life, in general.

Although the postpartum depression has lifted, I'm starting to feel like I'm living the life everyone else wants me to live. I'm not even sure what I want.

Jackson and I are just living parallel lives that don't really intersect. I'm just beginning to realize that Jackson puts his job—and my father—first, all the time. Looking back, I see that this has always been the case. I guess I enjoyed earning my father's approval when I first started dating Jackson and later married him. Sometimes, though, I wonder if I love him, or if I ever really loved him, at all.

We spend very little time together and, when we're in the same space, we don't have much to say to each other that doesn't revolve around our children or the company. I think Jackson—who's moved up through the company—seems to be expecting to be put in charge of my father's business when Dad retires.

One night when we were fighting, I accused Jackson of marrying me for this very reason. He dismissed it, saying maybe I should go back on my depression medication.

I'm getting angrier and angrier with him. I might have married Jackson partly to win my father's approval, but it isn't enough now.

Elise began pursuing Jackson as part of her role as the "good daughter" with her father. If this marriage is to become more than her proving herself to daddy, Elise needs to have a conversation with her husband about their relationship. If they both want this to work, Jackson needs to begin investing as much in the marriage as in his job and Elise needs to work on hearing what he wants from the relationship. Elise's parents wanted a "son" to work in their business and, through this, give them some continuity. When Elise married Jackson, she made them happy, but now she's got to think about what makes her happy.

The Bottom Line: Worry Only about What You Think

While trying to mend yourself through your relationships can be natural, there's much greater power in fixing yourself. Try finding a therapist or go to a self-help group. Then, realize that your power lies in your choices. Relationships are complicated and can be fulfilling, but they don't fill up the internal empty spaces.

Start Doing This

When you're looking at your relationship, don't judge or condemn yourself. Try to look at your situation with the kindness you'd have if you were thinking about a friend. You're not a bad person, and being objective about the relationship is easier if you aren't self-critical.

Determine the Real Reason You're in This Relationship   79

You Got Pregnant

Perhaps you're still in this relationship because you got pregnant. The scenarios are endless—maybe you'd just met the guy or had been dating him casually for years. Either way, you decided that keeping the pregnancy and working on a relationship with the father of your child seemed like the best choice. Without the child, you might not have seen him again.

You've made the best of the situation, and continued in a relationship that might have otherwise ended. The two of you have tried raising your child together, but the relationship is rough now. This doesn't mean you don't love him, but you have to decide whether this is a functional relationship for the two of you. It might be healthy to learn to work out the conflicts. It might also be best for both of you to move on.

Why Did You Want Him in the First Place?

If we can rule out alcohol as a factor, you need to look at why you got naked with the guy in the first place. Was he attractive? Did you like the way he laughed? Be honest with yourself. If you weren't so frustrated by what's happening between you now, would you still be attracted to him?

Wrong Reasons?
Even if you got with him for all the wrong reasons, he still may be good for you.

Allow the good stuff to register even if you've seriously thought about leaving him. He might have a nice body and know how to use it. He might still make you laugh. Add those to the "plus" column. It's important to be fair about this. This relationship has problems, but it might be worth fixing. As a matter of fact, you might be in this relationship because he can still turn you on. Whatever the good things are, recognize and acknowledge them.

The Bottom Line: It's Not Black-and-White

Shared parenthood isn't a reason for a relationship, but getting together because you were pregnant doesn't mean you don't have a chance. You may have more in common than a shared baby.

Brenna's Story:

With us, it was a classic story of a cocktail waitress and a bartender starting to date. I always thought Caleb was cute and I liked how he spent his breaks studying for his college courses. But I had a boyfriend back then and it wasn't until I found that guy cheating and kicked him to the curb that I ended up spending one whole night flirting with Caleb when we were both working the same shift. When he asked me to go home with him later, I had a reckless moment and just went. I figured this was a little gift I'd give myself.

Caleb and I spent one breathtaking night together. After that, things got a little weird. He made an awkward speech about how busy his life was. I said that after my last relationship, I needed to spend some time with my girlfriends, rather than hop from guy to guy. So, we both stepped back.

That lasted until I missed my second period. I'd tried to tell myself that missing the first one had to have been due to the stress of ending that relationship and finding a new apartment. But I was pregnant, and since Caleb was my only indulgence in the time period that counted, he had to be the father. When I told him, Caleb took it like a man. He put his school on a back burner and prepared to take responsibility for the baby.

After a few months of time spent together, Caleb proposed and I accepted him. It wasn't so bad. I really liked Caleb and had for a long time. When our daughter was born, we were both thrilled with being parents. We had both left our jobs at the bar and found other work; me in an insurance office and Caleb selling shoes at the mall. He worked his way up to assistant manager of the store and kept going to school in the evenings to earn his business degree.

But our relationship has rocky times, too, with us arguing over everything from what kind of diaper to buy to which friends we should hang out with. After a while, the arguments got more bitter and I started telling Caleb that we wouldn't have gotten together if I hadn't gotten pregnant.

We both love our daughter, but I've found myself feeling less and less like staying in what is becoming a bad situation. Caleb is a good father, but he isn't much of a husband.

Brenna and Caleb have never worked out the basics of talking to one another and listening to each others' complaints—they are having serious difficulties communicating. The initial spark was there and they may really be able to commit to one another aside from their child—but the enjoyment they shared in the beginning hasn't been nurtured. This couple has to decide if they want to invest in each other and build a relationship of caring about and listening to one another. This is a very personal question. No one gets to tell either of them that they "should" stay. The hard question that Brenna needs to ask herself (and the question you need to ask yourself) is, baby aside, does she love him?

He's a "Safe" Guy

Being an adult with all the responsibilities of a job and bills can be a daunting experience. If feel you need a place to escape the pressure, you may have looked for a guy who avoids risk and is a calming influence in your life. Avoiding risk might actually be part of your definition of love. It isn't a complete one, however. You need to see what your partner offers you beyond his security and reliability.

While it's nice to be with someone who makes you feel safe, that alone doesn't ensure a loving relationship. Consider these ideas:

- Relationships need to be safe. No matter why you got together, you should feel safe in the relationship.
- *Safe* doesn't always mean healthy.
- Certain kinds of "safe" can be boring.
- Dealing with relationship issues may be keeping the relationship interesting.
- Relationships aren't good hiding places. They need to be more than a place to hide.
- Don't sell yourself short. Believe in your capacity to handle life.

Few people like to argue with their mates, and that's one reason they may end up with a "safe" partner. And yes, it's upsetting to disagree with the person you're going to bed with, particularly when the disagreements are deep and divisive. You may have thought you could avoid this by investing in a default, "safe" relationship, but this kind of avoidance can leave you mired in your own issues. Without someone to present an opposite perspective, you aren't challenged to grow.

Long-term happiness and long-term personal benefit come from relationships in which you share similar values and have some challenge to grow. This challenge is most naturally presented by being in a relationship with a person who is *not like you*, who is not "safe."

Why Do You Need Safety?
There are two reasons people seek the safe relationship:

1. You had a rugged childhood, filled with risk and threat.
2. You feel you're really not capable of keeping yourself safe. This could be taken in the literal sense—maybe you're afraid

of being mugged—or in a more general sense, as in being afraid guys might take advantage of you.

While some children who've grown up amidst dangerous situations simply end up in dangerous relationship situations themselves, some deliberately seek relationship safe havens. Or, did you get into this relationship because you don't think you can handle life on your own? If you feel that way, you might try to find safety in everything—including your job or religion. Some individuals try hard to ensconce themselves into lifestyles that have no risk at all (think Meg Ryan in the movie *French Kiss*).

 Say This to Him
"We both deserve to be with someone who loves us and whom we love in return. That may or may not be something we can do for each other."

Do you feel like you're always making mistakes and that others frequently need to rescue you? You may have adopted this role in childhood for some reason. Perhaps a series of calamities might have followed you, bad choice after bad choice. It has some benefits, even if the disadvantages are clear. When you feel you can't handle things, other people to step in and save the day. You didn't have to negotiate the price of your car, tell a friend you couldn't come to her wedding, or find your own way home from the airport. (Of course, these "saviors" can become a greater danger than the stuff you didn't think you could handle, but that's not immediately obvious.)

The Bottom Line: Rely on Yourself for Safety

A "safe" guy would never cheat on you or fail to meet an obligation. Of course, these traits are greatly desirable, but they alone aren't enough of a basis for a strong relationship. Even the "safe" guy doesn't want you to stick with him just because he's not going to stray. There's an inference that he's so boring, no other woman will poach him.

> **Healthy Challenges**
> Having it all doesn't always feel good. Sometimes struggle opens the door for growth, even though the struggle itself can be very painful and difficult. The new skills, behaviors, and confidence that result from the struggle are what's worth remembering.

However, good relationships empower you, rather than protect you. Yes, there's a sheltering quality to a healthy relationship, but only in that it gives you a safe place to learn and grow. If you're staying in this relationship simply because he protects you from something you're afraid of (infidelity, bankruptcy, etc.), you're enabling yourself to continue to be afraid of those things. Instead, your partner should help you feel strong enough to take on those challenges.

He Was a Challenge

The real issue with dating and committing to a guy primarily because he's a "challenge" is that this relationship can be more about your needing to prove something to *yourself* than about being with him. We already discussed the impact of what happens if "landing" your partner helped you prove something to other people; now we're talking about this relationship proving something to yourself. If you dated the most popular high school jock or married the Warren Beatty of your office, you might be sticking it out because you don't want to surrender that victory.

Truly connecting with another person in a relationship needs to be about more than proving your attractiveness or finding a way to flex your flirting muscle. If you don't feel attractive or good enough, you need to work to raise your self-esteem and find specific ways to feel worthwhile. If you are able to feel confident on your own, you might see him differently.

If you got into this relationship because you were trying to conquer a challenge, or prove something to yourself, you now need to decide if you are willing to engage in developing a full relationship. You either need to invest emotionally in building the relationship or you need to leave him. There are better ways to prove yourself than being with a man you don't love.

You Have No Other Options

Staying in a relationship because you're afraid there's no one else for you out there is living in fear . . . plus, it's not true. If you are unhappy, you deserve better. This world is filled—let me say it again, *filled*—with single people of all ages trying to make a connection with another person. You have lots of other options, even though you may not think so. Your mate may have even told you that no other guy would want you. If so, he's wrong. Don't let this intimidation keep you in a place you don't want to be. You deserve someone who likes and loves you.

> ### *Perfection Doesn't = Love*
> Relationships aren't about beauty or being physically perfect. Beautiful women can have husbands who do lousy things. Even gorgeous, perfect women struggle with making it work. You don't need to be perfect to be happy.

You may think you're not pretty because you're overweight, or think you're not smart because you didn't finish your college degree. What you need to realize is that most guys aren't looking for perfection. They want to feel special and loved and important. They want to be respected and they want a woman who enjoys being with them.

This doesn't require you to be physically perfect or even completely emotionally strong. Every individual in this world has personal challenges yet everyone deserves love.

You Lack the Motivation to Leave

Inertia is a little-known issue in relationships that typically covers up fears and anxieties. Sometimes you stay because you just don't want to pack up the kitchen. You don't want to have to be single again. You don't want to deal with the hassles of dating. All understandable. But you may have to do it anyway, if you want to give yourself a chance to be happy.

Or, you can stay in this troubled relationship and you can keep being unhappy. You probably have days when it's not horrible, but staying just because you don't want to deal with getting out is selling yourself short. You deserve better.

If you can't seem to find another reason why you're still with your partner despite the fact that you're unhappy, consider this one. Struggling to find the will to leave doesn't necessarily mean that you're lazy or unmotivated in other areas of your life; it just means that you're not yet ready to face the challenge of starting over. If that's the case, ask yourself why. What are the things that you still love about him?

You're Staying Out of Habit

You may be accustomed to being in this relationship, but staying with him only for that reason cheats you out of developing an enjoyable relationship. As creatures of habit, human beings like things they know and can count on, but you must remember that unless these things have value and meaning, you simply become a slave to the habit. So, is the trouble serious enough to do something about? How bad is it? Can you fix things with him, or do you just need to move on? Looking at this can be painful and distressing, but it's important to examine these factors.

Here are some common ingrained habits of couples in troubled relationships:

- An unwillingness to deal with conflict
- Living with forced resignation
- Employing a "Don't ask what you don't want to know/Don't tell her anything she'll get upset about" methodology
- Being the "fake couple" for appearances only
- Having repeated arguments over the same problems with no resolution

Leaving, or asking him to leave, sounds final. It sounds easier to just stay. Don't give yourself a hard time for thinking this way. After all, the relationship isn't always bad. Maybe it's unhappy more often than not, but sometimes things are okay. While you tell yourself you stay out of comfort and habit, you might really be anxious about ending the relationship. Leaving the "known" involves big change. You might have an anxiety that you'll never again find someone to love you, and that can make it just seem easier to stay with what you know. You might be buying into the idea that no one will ever love you the way you want to be loved. Habits sometimes cloak feelings you don't feel you can confront.

You're Afraid of the Dating Scene

Are you staying because you're afraid of the dating scene? You might be if any of these thoughts cross your mind:

- You might think you'll do crazy things with men you don't know well.
- You might be afraid of dating and disease.
- You won't know which guy you can trust.

These are all normal fears, but that doesn't mean you can't make a good life for yourself. Is your current relationship helping you to be a better person? This is what a good relationship does.

You're Simply Afraid

Fear is a lousy reason to stay, whether it's fear for yourself or fear for him. You might be afraid of being alone or not being able to support yourself or your kids. You might be afraid to leave him, wondering if your former mate will fall apart without you. You want him to be okay, even if you're not sure you want to stay with him. Maybe he won't function without you or he'll never find another relationship. If you're staying because of this anxiety, you're forgetting to believe in yourself and in him. Caring for someone—even if you can't live together—means having some faith in him. He can function. He may not choose to, but that's more about him than about you.

Recognize Your Positive Steps

For some people, the reason they're still in the relationship is obvious. But this chapter may have forced you to take a hard look at your behavior and childhood and realize the deeper connection between your partner and your own needs, whether obvious or hidden. Even though it's difficult, being honest with yourself is a vital part of deciding whether to stay or go. Don't undervalue the progress you made simply by thinking about past mistakes, uncomfortable realities, and real feelings.

If you feel like you've given this relationship all you can, your initial reason for coming together may begin to feel less and less significant. On the other hand, if you can still identify with the initial reasons, you may have something worth saving.

- **You should stay if:** You're in this relationship because you think it's good for you, even though it's hard.
- **You should leave if:** You're only in the relationship because you don't want to upset others or because you don't think anyone else will love you.

Exercises and Affirmations

Give yourself some time alone to think about what you want. Think about what makes you happy and notice whether there are big things—career, physical condition, or family issues—outside the relationship that may be influencing your perception. Is your discontent really due to the relationship, or are you actually unhappy with other areas that seem harder to change?

After you do that, take a full weekend (or a single day or afternoon) to do your favorite activities. Treat yourself like you're recovering from the flu. After your retreat, you can go back to trying to sort out the relationship. You've taken a hard look at yourself in this chapter, and it's important to replenish your spirit with some pampering.

Above all, forgive yourself for the reasons you got into this relationship, particularly if they look unhealthy.

chapter six

You *Can* Make Your Life Better

Things to Consider

- You can't help others if you can't help yourself. It's like putting on your own air mask first in an airplane. Taking care of yourself will help you take care of your relationship.
- You can't judge your own strength by whether or not you *feel* strong. Remember, feelings aren't always a complete reality.
- Others won't always like your taking care of yourself and believing in yourself. Carry on anyway.
- Leaving the relationship doesn't always mean leaving your problems.

The decision to stay or go can be daunting. Perhaps what's most daunting about the decision is that you have to make it alone. But that's the only way it can be done to ensure that you make the best decision for yourself. Only *you* can assess whether or not this relationship is good for you or whether you can find a way to make it better. No one else gets to decide what's best for you. The most important thing to remember as you face this challenge is that you're strong enough and fully equipped to make this choice. If at any point you feel inadequate and overwhelmed, remind yourself that you *can* make the choice that's right for you. Sometimes, it's just a matter of believing in yourself.

Quiz: Assessing Your Self-Confidence

On a scale of one to five (with one meaning you disagree strongly and five meaning you agree strongly), answer the following questions:

1. You have low self-esteem. _____
2. You think you should stay because you aren't sure you're making the right choice if you decide to leave. _____
3. You're listening to others' opinions, rather than your own. _____
4. You don't think you make good decisions. _____
5. You're afraid you'll regret whatever choice you make. _____

If you scored 20 or more points: You're having trouble believing in your own strength.

If you scored 11–19 points: You have difficulty realizing you can make good decisions.

If you scored 5–10 points: Your sense of self isn't strong and probably isn't accurate.

Feelings Versus Thoughts

Before discussing self-worth and self-belief, it's important to understand the difference between feeling and thinking. They aren't the same thing. You may *feel* like an idiot for getting a speeding ticket, but getting caught by a police officer doesn't mean you have limited intellect at all. Just because you may *feel* stupid, doesn't mean you *are*. Look at these examples:

- **Feelings:** mad, sad, guilty, happy, anxious, fearful, and so on
- **Thoughts:** "I'm such an idiot"; "He wouldn't have cheated if I was a better wife"; "I could leave him"

Thoughts and feelings are very different. We all have both, although feelings aren't very visible in some people, and thoughts aren't the basis for some people's decisions. The fact remains that all humans need both. Don't doubt yourself because you have strong feelings or because these feelings influence your choices. You need to recognize your thoughts and your emotions to make the decisions that will help you feel strong.

What Is Self-Worth?

Even intelligent, attractive people struggle with believing in themselves, particularly when their relationships aren't working well. You might think if you were thinner or had a higher educational degree, things would be better between the two of you. It wouldn't—because "things" don't have the power to make you feel better about yourself. Only you have that power. It may seem that if you were *really* worthwhile, you'd make fewer mistakes and be more self-confident. Your relationship wouldn't be this difficult if you were prettier, more on the ball, or more dedicated. You might think that if you were a smarter person you'd feel less like an idiot for not knowing how to make things work between you and your partner.

Not true. Even though you mess up at times, you're still worth loving. Relationships are tremendously difficult for even the most intelligent, most beautiful, most *together* people.

Supermodels and schoolteachers alike have a hard time believing in themselves and have questionable relationships. Relationship troubles run through pretty much every demographic and can be partly attributed to the fact that life is sometimes messy, complicated, and difficult. These challenges can lead to self-doubt and even self-condemnation. Don't give in to the urge to blame yourself for everything.

> ### You Could Be Wrong
> How you feel about yourself is based on what you believe. What you believe may not be *true*.

One of the first steps in developing a healthy sense of self-worth in a relationship is to conduct a self-assessment. What do you really think about yourself? And how accurate are you?

Conduct a Self-Assessment

As you weigh your thoughts and feelings about your decision to stay or go, look at yourself with some objectivity. This is very difficult to do. Your objective assessment is likely something different from how you *feel* about yourself. For example, you may objectively say, "I have a college degree and a good job," but you may still *feel* stupid when it comes to certain decisions. It's not easy to be objective about yourself. Your feelings about yourself are a result of what you believe about yourself—it's almost as if you're drawing a line from cause to effect. For example, your grades were never as good as your sister's, so as a result, you ended up believing you're not as smart as she is. If you believe you're not really intelligent, you might feel stupid in some situations. To get you started, think about the following questions:

1. What are your strong points? You're used to what you do well, but others probably struggle in ways you don't.

2. What are your weakest areas? Where do you struggle, and in what ways do you need to grow?
3. Would your best friend agree with this? Is your assessment an objective one?

You need both feelings and thoughts, but you're better off if you don't make decisions based purely on feelings. On the other hand, your thoughts about yourself and your mate will lead you astray if they aren't accurate. You need to determine how accurate your thoughts are. Since feelings and emotions are triggered by what you believe about a situation or a relationship, you need to be as clear in your self-assessment as possible.

Step outside yourself as if you were an unconcerned observer. Ask yourself what you'd say about a good friend in the same circumstances. Maybe some of your friends have even been in this situation or done similar things in relationships. Did you judge them as harshly as you judge yourself? Typically, it's easier for you to see mitigating circumstances for someone else than for yourself.

Start Doing This
Do your best to step back and try to look at yourself fairly. This isn't the moment to beat yourself up. You aren't evil incarnate; you're just a person like everyone else. Give yourself a break.

Looking at yourself objectively doesn't mean sugarcoating. You're not automatically wonderful and always healthy and functional in your choices. Sometimes, you screw up. Everyone does, but you don't mess up all the time, and probably not as often as you think you do.

Consider Others' Views of You

Your own view of yourself isn't the only one around. All your life, you've had voices—parents, teachers, friends, bosses—telling you about yourself. Along the way, you've absorbed some of these and taken them as truth when some of them are dead wrong.

There is some value in discovering how others see you, however. The key is that you can't always listen to the ones who are heavily invested in loving or hating you, such as your partner or your mother. Instead, ask an objective friend about you—ask him or her to be really honest. Some friends will be able to do this for you. (Others don't want to hurt your feelings and will always support whatever they think you want, but some people will try to be honest with you, even if that means what they say may hurt.) Asking several objective people their view of your situation can give you more perspective. Just be careful whom you ask, and do your very best to listen.

Please note, this is not a suggestion to take a poll. You don't need to question multiple, random people, asking them what they *really* think about you. That's embarrassing for everyone. You need to think about what you've already been told about yourself. If no one tells you anything, directly or indirectly, you might want to look at the possibility that you're pretty closed off or you're just not listening. You may be sending out some serious "Don't Come Close" signals if you truly don't want to hear what others think. People generally make direct or indirect remarks about individuals who they think might care.

Approach the Conversation with an Open Mind

Before you speak with anyone else about your situation, try to clear your head of preconceived notions. You need to be able to hear others' assessment of you without dismissing them by thinking, *They just don't know the* real *me*. It's natural to think that your partner knows you the best—he'll probably tell you that, in fact—but it may not be true. You can find a more complete view of yourself by looking at the opinions of those you respect. Even if everyone in your life has their own set of problems, chances are, they'll still have a more objective view of you than you do.

Who to Ask

Ideally, it's great to get an opinion from a disinterested person. Not from people who don't care about the situation at all, but those who aren't invested in whatever relationship decision you may make. In other words, not your mother, your best friend, or the clergyman who dipped your infant in the font. Someone who knows you, but who can be fair. This is when a good therapist can be of help—but therapists aren't your only option.

There may be other people in your life who'll level with you. Be careful, though. Hidden agendas can be a problem, even with people you know and trust. You may have a trusted relative or friend who'll level with you. Even a coworker who knows you well can be of help. Remember, you need to hear what's offered, not ask for feedback and then defend yourself.

Look Back at Your Childhood

Everyone is impacted by the people who played a significant role in their childhood. Whether you believed whatever people said about you or to you or rejected their opinions entirely, you've still been impacted. You couldn't *not* be affected by the people around you in your youth.

It's important to be able to find some objectivity about the folks who raised you so you can better gauge the accuracy of their assessment of you. It doesn't matter if you grew up in a loving, nurturing, intact family unit (the Huxtables), or in a succession of foster homes, or somewhere in between—everyone needs this reality check. Your beliefs about yourself and your character were built in the context of your childhood experiences. You were young and your brain was like a sponge. You picked up what was there to pick up.

Whoever raised you probably did their best, but they had issues, too. Factor those into what they said about you. For example, if your parent had a cleanliness fetish, your comfort with clutter might have been seen as a character flaw. (It's not. Some people file; others stack.) I'm not necessarily blaming your parents, but your early experiences strongly affected your self-esteem.

If you're different from what your parents wanted you to be, you may have grown up with a sense of low self-worth. You might have tried to do what they wanted of you and failed. Or you may have rebelled and decided to be the opposite of what was expected. If your self-worth is tied to earning your parents' approval or rejection, you might need to redefine who you want to be.

It's not always easy to see if you were correct in your assessment of their expectations. Were these your interpretation of what they wanted, or were you actually told what was expected of you? You may have understood something they didn't mean to convey. An adult conversation—if you have these with the adults from your youth—might be called for.

You *Are* a Worthy Person

Once you have a sense of your current state of mind and an understanding of what shaped your view of yourself, you can begin to work on boosting your self-confidence. Many women in less-than-perfect relationships have low self-esteem. It's very difficult to get rid of a nagging feeling that you're not good enough. Even if friends and family tell you that you're a great person and you generally trust their opinions, you probably still doubt yourself. So, how do you see yourself differently? Train yourself to see your inherent goodness.

Do you need to move to an undeveloped country, work with the poorest, most ill individuals, or give all your worldly goods to the less fortunate in order to be a "good" person? No.

Personal worth can be defined by excellence of character or as having qualities that are valued by others. You could say that an individual is worthy if she can be useful or helpful to another person or to the world. This definition is very broad and can be embodied in a gesture as simple as smiling at the people you pass. **You are worthwhile**, whether you feel it or not. If you don't feel a sense of self-worth, your challenge is to figure out why.

Personal Worth in Terms of Power

In addition to personal worth, which all individuals have (even if they don't recognize it on their own), you should experience personal *power* in your life as well. Do you know how to get what you want? Can you assess whether you want reasonable things? Can you handle life? Are you able to cope with personal challenges with some level of ethics most of the time?

You may point to times when you don't deal with the crap in your life as reinforcement of your assessment of yourself as lousy. Maybe you call in sick to work if you're stressed out, then eat a bag of cookies and spend the day watching talk shows and *Judge Judy*. Not a particularly productive way to handle stress, some would say—but having a day or two like this doesn't mean you're not worthy or strong. It just means you've been overwhelmed, swamped, by life.

Assessing Your Personal Worth

Let's get a sense of how you view your personal worth. Ask yourself the following questions:

1. Do I have a hard time seeing my own strengths?
2. Can I see the areas in which I need to develop?

3. Do I beat myself up for these areas?
4. Does my partner see my good points?

Assessing your personal worth is challenging because it requires a certain objectivity (that word again!) and it's difficult to be objective about yourself. That said, this task is easy for one reason: **Having personal worth is like having brain activity. You have it; it's just a matter of finding it.** You were born worthy. It's something you have to work *not* to have. If you are a serial killer, you've probably abdicated any claim to personal worth. Otherwise, you sometimes stumble, just like everyone else.

Even if you do angry, vindictive things; even if you yell at your kids—you're still worthy. Yes, doing these things will make you feel lousy, and that comes with the territory. It's life's way of indicating when you've gone off course, like rumble strips on the highway.

Individuals who identify themselves as struggling with personal worth usually don't see their own successes. You see your mistakes much more easily (flashing strobe lights) than your successes (little match in the dark). Since the point of this exercise is to discover your self-worth, force yourself to think about what you have done right. Take note of your good points for a week. Look for these moments—you *will* find them if you look seriously. It'll be eye-opening.

Ways to Develop Personal Power

Developing personal power starts with having the guts to look at your mistakes, but that's just part of it. You must look at your mistakes and face adversity in your own life. Doing so will increase your sense of personal power.

Face Challenges Directly

The hard part about increasing your personal power is having the courage to face tough situations. No one wants to do this—

talking to the professor who seems to hate you, owning up to your mistakes with your partner, admitting to a personal flaw or habit that's causing trouble. Facing the issue feels bad, but it takes such personal integrity that you'll feel stronger and more capable once you've done it.

The only effective way to build self-esteem is by proving to yourself that you can handle scary, bad situations. You can have challenging relationship conversations. You can survive a divorce or a breakup or even being cheated on. You can.

Know That It's Okay to Screw Up

Looking back at your mistakes can be challenging, but you need to do so in order to learn from them. Typically, people beat themselves up for the wrong things. Every now and then, however, you make a clear misstep that you should learn from. Maybe you cheated on your boyfriend when you were mad at him or you got so drunk you took off your shirt and danced on a bar. Whatever you did, it was probably embarrassing and you shudder when you think about it.

News flash: Everyone screws up. It's not just you. Unfortunately, it's part of life. The most important thing is being able to learn from your screwups.

> ### *Bad Choices Don't Make People Bad*
> Never, ever believe you're bad. People usually aren't bad. They just get confused and mixed up and make bad choices. This doesn't mean they're worthless people, though.

Look at your mistakes—boldly and without hiding from them— and see what you could have done differently. Failure is not in the messing up. Real failure is in not learning from your ineffective, damaging, or hurtful behavior. Remember, screwing up does not mean you are not worthwhile. You are worthy, even if you make mistakes.

Truly Understand Your Mistakes

Although it's okay to make mistakes, don't be too quick to forgive your own mistakes—or his. Being too fast with the forgiveness button usually means you just don't want to deal with the problem. You want to pretend it didn't happen or you try to insist to yourself that it definitely won't happen again. It's too painful, too scary. You want it behind you.

However, if you grant forgiveness without understanding why you made a particular mistake, the following things happen:

- You stay in the wrong. You can't get out of this with a simple "it's over!"
- You make the same mistakes over and over.
- The "forgiveness" (manufactured without understanding) doesn't convey the benefits of truly understanding another person.

Quick forgiveness is a snare and a delusion. Don't believe it. Genuine forgiveness doesn't work this way. Immediate forgiveness isn't really forgiveness—it's dodging the issues.

More important than forgiveness in building personal strength is understanding why you made the mistake. You need to see what happened before you can forgive yourself for it. Understanding will help you improve self-honesty and will also help if you're dealing with others' bad behavior.

Take Care of Yourself

You're strong and you can survive mistakes and challenges, but you need to take care of yourself. See your own needs. This is really important for developing personal strength. You need to make sure you're getting the basics—like sleep and exercise. It's important to know if someone is truly listening to you. This is your right, particularly if you're in an intimate relationship. You deserve to have your significant other listen to you. You also have a right to a life outside of him. Friends. Relatives. It's not okay to have one set of rules for you and another for him.

You Can Do It

Even if you feel overwhelmed, ambivalent, scared, and unsure, you can deal with this situation. Relationship conflict is difficult for everyone. Feeling weak doesn't mean you're weak. You can act. You have the capacity to sort through relationship realities. Listen to him, by actually *hearing* him, as you learned to do in Chapter 3. Repeat back to him what he has said to you, so he knows you heard him.

> ### Don't Talk Yourself into Being the Problem
> If you believe you should have made your mate feel better about himself or you should have done *blah, blah, blah*—then you'll feel responsible for the relationship conflict. You'll feel bad about yourself, and you probably don't deserve to feel that way.

Remember that you can change what you need to change. You can choose different actions, take different steps, say different things. You can behave differently—listen rather than react, bring up your conflicts openly, tell him what you like about him and what you need from him. All these actions are in your power and within your capacity to change. It's difficult to swallow your immediate, automatic reaction and instead think about how you're going to react. It's hard, but you can do it.

What You Should Tell Him

You also can change what you accept from him. Sometimes individuals tolerate as much bad stuff from their partners as they hand out. However, no one deserves to be called names or ignored. Your partner should have ways to communicate that don't involve the threat of leaving. Tell him that. Tell him that you need him to be different—to call you when he's coming home late, to treat your kids the same as he treats his own kids, to talk to you without yelling. Whatever. You are changing yourself. You'll need some changes from him, too.

 Say This to Him
"*There are times I don't like you, but I love you. I don't want anything bad to happen to you.*"

Love involves change for the better. If the relationship is good and functional, you'll change. So will he. Remember that you can use your power to adjust your behavior. You can learn from your failures and, in doing so, change both yourself and the relationship.

Recognize Your Positive Steps

Accepting your inherent self-worth and increasing your sense of personal power are key steps to making yourself a priority in your life. Treat yourself better and you'll be able to see your needs more clearly. When you can see your needs, the decision that's right for you might make itself clearer.

Recognizing your good qualities doesn't mean you're conceited. It doesn't mean you can't see your faults. It simply means that you know you are a great person and that you are capable of handling whatever life throws your way. You may make mistakes, but you'll learn from them. You may need help, so you'll ask for it. You may need to change and you may need your partner to change. All of these things are possible with a strong sense of personal power. You are making significant progress if you can identify the things that make you a good person and have the courage to face problems.

- **You should stay if:** You decide you can change some of your choices to make this relationship better.
- **You should go if:** This relationship is costing you more emotionally than it's bringing you.

> ### *Making Changes*
> Intimate relationships are an agreement between two people. Both have the option to walk away. In order for the relationship to prosper, both have to invest.

Exercises and Affirmations

When anxiety or worry pops up, envision pushing it out of your head like you'd push a heavy piece of furniture on sliders. Replace it with clear statements of your capacity. Remind yourself of all that you handle: job responsibilities, your children's lives, or your checkbook. Keep looking until you find an area where you're doing well. Yes, you're doing well somewhere. Inhale good air and exhale bad self-talk.

Don't tell your friends all the things he does wrong in order to bolster your own confidence in yourself. Your confidence is self-generated; it doesn't come from putting others down. When you have the urge to talk down to him, remind yourself that you're feeling anxious, and that's completely normal. Take confidence from your own actions.

part ii

should you stay?

chapter seven

Remembering Why You Fell for Him

Things to Consider

- Do you dislike him because you dislike yourself when you're with him? Perhaps you drink to cover unhappiness. Maybe he discourages you from achieving something you've always wanted to do.
- Do you like him but, deep down, you don't think he likes you?
- When you look back objectively, were you deluded about what you thought you saw in him in the beginning?

When you first met him, he was probably really on his game. He may have seemed interesting or smart or funny—whatever you were looking for in a guy. You loved him and he was wonderful. Now as the relationship seems to be crumbling all around you, it's important to remember why you fell for this guy. (You did fall for him. You probably even committed to spending your life with him.) Losing perspective on how you got here can mean you're likely to end up in a similar situation, either with him again or with another guy who seems like a repeat.

It's easy now to think that you were wrong about him back in the beginning. The whole relationship was a *mistake*, you might want to insist. After all, he probably doesn't seem all that terrific to you now. But if you're planning to try to rebuild the relationship, going back to its foundation helps you remember how you built it in the first place.

Quiz: What Has Changed?

On a scale of one to five (with one meaning you disagree strongly and five meaning you agree strongly), answer the following questions:

1. He's nothing like the guy you fell for. _____
2. The things you liked in him aren't there anymore. _____
3. You don't ever laugh with him now. _____
4. You now want very different lives. _____
5. He hardly ever understands you. _____

If you scored 20 or more points: You two have completely forgotten why you fell in love in the first place.

If you scored 11–19 points: You still think the reasons you fell in love with him are valid, but they've been lost amidst the conflict and fighting.

If you scored 5–10 points: You still have a lot in common with the couple who fell in love in the first place.

What Did You Tell Others?

If your relationship has deteriorated to the point that you can't remember what you ever saw in him, ask yourself what you told your mother, your sisters, or your friends about him. Maybe it was something like:

- He's hot
- He's funny
- He's reliable
- He's kind
- He's crazy, but in a good way

Make a list of the attributes you remember telling others about when you met him. Keep this list by you as you read the rest of the chapter. Let's take a look at some qualities you may have written down.

Amy's Story:

I thought he was hot, but Nathan dated a lot of other girls when we started working together. I'd just been hired as an engineer at his firm and I got the word pretty quickly that he was a *dog*. He had different women picking him up for lunch every other day and he got a hundred e-mails every day from women, and some of them were pretty racy. The techs used to talk about it.

I wasn't a hermit, either, and I had a boyfriend at the time. After that boyfriend and I broke up, I guess Nathan and I just happened to both eye each other at the same time. It turned out that we were both big hockey fans. So, we went to a few games together and yelled at the refs and our relationship just grew from there.

We started spending all our free time together. We both liked gross-out humor and hot dogs. All that was nice, but it was really hot in the sack for us. I liked that he knew what I was talking about when I was tearing my hair out at work. He didn't get upset at my friendly relationship with all the traffic cops in the area. I like to drive fast.

Sometimes, we argued over who did the laundry or who went to get the takeout, but it was manageable. Then, things went crazy at work. We had a new boss come into the firm and the guy really didn't like me from the start.

For some reason, though, the boss guy thought Nathan was the best. Nathan couldn't do any wrong with this guy, whereas I was always wrong. It put a lot of strain on us because Nathan saw all this guy's good qualities and, because the boss was always giving me a hard time, I couldn't see anything nice about him.

When this guy gave Nathan a promotion, I just lost it. It wasn't that I wanted that job. I just knew that now Mr. Boss and Nathan were going to be even greater buddies. After all, they were on the same team. But I was having a rough time and Nathan was not very supportive.

I finally got so fed up with Mr. Boss that I left and got a job at another company doing something similar. For a while, Nathan would still talk all admiring about my former boss. Then, he just stopped talking about anything that happened at his work, at all, even though I knew all the people he worked with. He didn't tell me when one group was getting laid off. Nothing!

Then it was like we didn't really talk about anything anymore. Not even hockey. We just aren't connecting.

It's like we were so caught up in talking about the work conflict that we didn't see the other issues between us. We get into big fights over silly stuff and it doesn't seem like we have any fun anymore.

I love Nathan, but we just can't get along.

Amy and Nathan need to have a conversation about the relationship, and work at really listening to one another's perspective. Jobs come and go, but relationships don't have to. Nathan may like the fact that his boss likes him, but he needs to quit defending the boss—even in his head—just as he doesn't need to let Amy bitch about Mr. Boss. Nathan does need, though, to listen to her *feelings* about her work. He needs to see her relief and excitement at her new job as not being a rejection of him and the old job. On the other hand, Amy needs to learn to relate to Nathan's experience, even though she felt differently working there.

The Attractive Character Traits You First Loved

The spark that brought you two together may have been based on some of the positive characteristics of his personality. You liked his smile. You thought he was bright. He made you laugh. Whatever the reason, you decided he was worth your time. Even if your relationship has hit a rough patch, these reasons may still be valid—they're just hovering under the surface of all the conflict.

He Made You Laugh

Maybe you fell in love with him, in part, simply because he made you laugh. There's something powerful about shared laughter. It leaves a sense of connection, of being bonded. Does he still make you laugh? Think about the last time the two of you had fun together, and try to repeat that event as often as you can. Spending time having fun together can get you through some difficult times.

> *It Can Be True . . .*
> - Opposites really do attract.
> - You may offer a really important perspective to your mate if he is very different from you.
> - Everyone has to learn to communicate in a relationship . . . even if both partners come from very similar backgrounds.

Laughing together is a powerful aphrodisiac, too. Enjoying him so much may have blinded you to issues that now seem too big to overcome, but in the moment, a guy who makes you laugh is already a step ahead of the pack.

He Was Reliable

You might have—once you got to know him—been attracted to your mate's work ethic. While not as sexy as shared laughter, this attribute can be powerful. It can give a sense of security, knowing that the guy you're with can always get a job and hold up his end of the financial responsibilities. If you want kids and choose to stay home from work with them for a couple of years, this guy can handle the mortgage. He may still be someone you can count on despite your current difficulties.

He Was/Is Hot

There's always the possibility, too, that when you met him you thought he was smokin' hot. You may have shaken his hand and thought instantaneously about how you could get him alone and get you both naked. Sexual attraction is a powerful force and, when it's present, many other aspects of a relationship, such as whether you have similar life goals or values, fade.

> *In the Beginning . . .*
> Somehow, when you met him, he met a need you had. Maybe you weren't wrong about that part of him.

Even if you didn't like his mother, his dog, or his work ethic, wanting *him* may have drawn you into the relationship. Hot sex won't keep a relationship running on its own, but it sure can be the reason you were first attracted to him.

He's So Nice!

Maybe your partner has a big heart, and that may have warmed you to him right away. If he didn't make fun of your friend who sang karaoke really badly or he didn't mind that you ran errands for your mother, you may have decided right away that he was just a good guy—even more so if *he* ran errands for your mother. Perhaps he was loyal, caring, and kind.

If the two of you are in crisis, he may not seem particularly kind right now. You might be of a very different opinion about his *kindness*, but you need to remember the man he was when you first met him. Those traits are still a part of him. If he has a heart of gold, don't overlook it.

Why You Actually Fell in Love

Remember that tingly feeling when you first realized you were in love with him? That's important as you work on this relationship now. Though his character traits may have initially brought you two together, the following reasons may have helped you fall in love.

He Liked You

If you're in a relationship, someone must have liked someone. Don't underestimate the power of being liked. When you find out someone likes you, it's very natural to find yourself liking him back. Who doesn't want to feel desirable and needed?

If you're now second-guessing why you liked him back, consider the following questions.

ASK YOURSELF:
1. Has the unresolved conflict between us made me forget that I liked him in the beginning?
2. Am I struggling to be fair to him?
3. Can I see why *other women* would find him attractive?
4. Don't I have unlikable moments, too?

The only way to make a good, solid decision about what to do next with this relationship is to look at the entire thing—including the beginning and your own qualities, good and bad.

You're a Little Weird

Very few of us are without some strange habit. There are things about you that aren't average. (Oddly, most of us aren't average.) This guy not only didn't mind your strange side; he liked it and encouraged you to be yourself.

You Fell . . . Even Though He Wasn't Your Type

Relationships between two people who'd never have thought they fit together can sometimes really work. Balancing out one another is a gift these kinds of relationships offer. That doesn't mean you don't run into trouble—lots of people do. Remember, relationships are incredibly hard. But, in the beginning, you might have loved that he was very different from the guys you usually dated. Something about that difference was attractive back then. Try to recapture what it was.

Maybe You Didn't Fall . . .

Sometimes you end up in a relationship you didn't plan on. Whether you got pregnant or your parents arranged a marriage for you, this may not have originally been a relationship you expected.

> *The Child Factor*
> Having kids won't make your marriage stronger. In fact, having children places marriages under big stress.

However, there must be a reason why you stayed in the relationship long enough to find yourself here, considering whether or not to leave. If you wanted out right away, you would've left a long time ago. So why did you stay this long? There must be part of this relationship that you still enjoy and value.

He Understood!

You may have been deeply involved in time-consuming volunteering with your church when the two of you first met. Or you were in a surgical residency program that barely allowed you to breathe, or you were on a cell tower construction crew and risked your life daily. You might have had a crazy life and you loved that he was supportive of you.

 Say This to Him
"I'm trying to be the person you used to like. I'm trying to remember all the things I liked about you, too."

He didn't get all bent out of shape when you couldn't return his calls immediately. He understood that you were working toward a goal—a prized job or a cushy retirement bonus or developing an important skill. He knew what this meant to you. He might have been supportive in all the ways that count. He did your laundry. He got takeout for your supper. He didn't gripe when you couldn't go to his mother's birthday party. He seemed to know you loved him, even when you didn't know how to say it. Having a supportive lover can warm the cockles of your heart.

So, is he still a warm lover? Think about the last time he did something special for you or you did something for him. These moments occur naturally in a relationship when you both feel valued and important to one another.

Grace's Story:

We met at the worst time. I'd just been given a big promotion at my work and part of the deal was that I whip a division into shape. It was both exciting and scary, at the same time. I'd wanted this opportunity for a long time and, now that I had it, I didn't want to blow it. But this was a huge job. I had over a hundred personnel to direct, and most of them acted like they had no clue how they were expected to perform.

I told Ethan all this on our first date. I found him very attractive, but I just had no time to give a relationship right then. But instead of taking me at my word and going away, Ethan hung in there. He brought me flowers, didn't get upset when I had to cancel dates at the last minute, and listened to me rant about the crazy people I was trying to work with. And all the time, he kept telling me that he knew I could do this. It was unbelievable how supportive he was.

The first time he said I could do it, I'd just left a meeting with my managers that was so frustrating I wanted to scream. I remember absorbing his sincere words and then taking him back to my bedroom for some much needed R & R. I was really touched by his faith in me and by the fact that he didn't seem to need me to tell him how I was feeling all the time.

That was five years ago, and I ended up making my goals with the company. Ethan and I are still together now, but we're struggling. He's had a career change recently, and I went through an unexpected health scare. I know we still love each another, but lately the joy seems to have gone out of being together. We still live together and go through the motions of having a relationship, but I don't seem to know how to connect with Ethan these days. I find myself answering work e-mails while he's trolling the Internet for different jobs. We're just very far apart these days and I almost wish we could go back to the crazy insanity of those first days. At least then, I felt important to him.

Grace and Ethan were strongly attracted in the beginning of their relationship, but they never developed a healthy way to resolve issues. While she initially liked that Ethan didn't need her to talk about her feelings, if Grace wants the relationship to continue, she needs to invest herself in it. She needs to tell Ethan how she feels, not just once or twice, but on an ongoing basis. She originally fell in love with him due partly to his supportiveness when she was in a stressful time. With his job challenge, Ethan needs her to be supportive of him now. They might not have the same manner of expressing or absorbing emotional support, but both need it and both need to give it to one another.

Relationships Need:
- Supportiveness
- Mutuality (you should be equal partners)
- Expression of emotion (more than a quickie and a peck on the cheek before you leave)
- Conflict resolution skills (can't say that strongly enough). Review Chapter 3.

You Shared Mutual Goals

Maybe the two of you worked side-by-side on the same huge lawsuit. Maybe he was working toward the same goal you sought—partnership at the big firm, a degree that required you to sacrifice all personal time, or trying to save a family business. If the two of you were caught up in the same whirlwind, you probably felt understood. If the two of you had the same goals, you shared a common commitment, not just to each other, but to one another's goals.

Shared goals can be powerful while you're striving for them, but once you've graduated or made that deal or achieved whatever the two of you were seeking, the relationship might be over. Before you walk away, look at whether the relationship can shift with you.

> ### Goals Can't Be Your Only Connection
> Similar goals can pull you close together, but they can't be your only connection. Find a connection beyond going after something you both want . . . after all, you're planning on getting there one day. What'll happen to the relationship after you're through celebrating?

The Lure of the Chase

There's something hot and powerful about chasing and then getting what you want. If that's the basis of the relationship you're in, ask yourself why. Maybe you were the one running and he finally caught you, but doesn't seem all that interested now that you're his. Either way, this relationship needs some bones—some solid, continuing benefit for both of you. If the lure of the hunt got you into this relationship (one way or another), and you haven't just moved on to the next "goal," ask yourself what else you're getting from it now.

You need to figure out what it meant to you when you first caught him. Was there some sense of pride for you? Did you think it meant you were sexy and powerful? You might have gotten off on the challenge. The problem is that this reason alone is pretty hollow. If you examine your feelings, you might care more for the hunted than you originally thought. You might have chased him originally for the rush of *getting* him, but perhaps now he's more than an object to be chased.

If, on the other hand, you were the hunted, you need to sift through this relationship thoroughly to find the real value between the two of you. It may not be obvious. If you find that your mate has no desire to be with you for who you are, ask yourself why you're still here.

Don't Fall for the *I Never Really Loved Him* Fallacy

Lots of people—when in the midst of relationship hell—want to believe that they never really loved this person. They certainly don't feel loving now. After a recent conflict, it's common to think you must have been crazy to get with this guy in the first place. Don't write him off without giving the beginning of your relationship some serious thought.

As we've discussed in this chapter, just because you're struggling now doesn't mean those things don't still count. You need to remember this and factor it into the decision you're trying to make.

Recognize Your Positive Steps

When you're distressed in a relationship, remembering the reasons you first fell for a guy can be difficult. By letting yourself revisit these emotions, you're believing in yourself and you're preparing yourself to move forward. If you deny or reject your initial feelings, you're simply falsifying the record to suit your current mood.

It might be that the reason you now dislike him a lot and think he'll never change is that you're just done with this relationship. Only you can decide when you have given it all you can. Lots of people may be offering commentary and advice, but only you truly know when there's still something left that's worth fighting for and when the relationship is dead.

- **You should stay if:** You'd fall in love with this same guy all over again.
- **You should leave if:** The relationship was based on something other than love, and love never developed when the two of you were together.

Exercises and Affirmations

Try to be as fair to yourself as you've been trying to be to him. Make a list of all the reasons *he* fell for *you*. Once you've finished your list, do something that's moderately risky for you. Take an oil painting class or learn Tae Bo or speak at a poetry slam. Believe in yourself enough to get out of your box. This chapter asks you to remember your early feelings for your partner, and confirms that showing yourself you can do something new strengthens your faith in yourself.

chapter eight

What You Can't Change

Things to Consider

- Are your differences really about the values you hold?
- Do you have personality differences you're having a hard time working through?
- Are you trying to hold on to a relationship when he's already emotionally left? If you're trying to hang on to part of the relationship, maybe you're not through with it. Ask yourself why.

Though we've talked a lot about both partners having to change in order to work through problems in the relationship, certain things won't—and shouldn't—change. A person's core values and beliefs are fundamental parts of who she is, and no amount of relationship strife will alter them. Knowing what will stay the same will help you understand what he won't be able to change as you two work on your relationship. What can change, however, is how you communicate and compromise about these issues. Read on to discover what parts of a person you can't change and how that fact may impact the future of your relationship.

Values

We've talked about values—these are the things and relationships about which you care the most. If you and your partner have significant conflicts about your different values, the relationship usually won't work. Why? Because *values aren't easily changed and they certainly can't be changed by someone else.* Conflicting values make for very difficult relationships and tend to leave issues without a solution. Neither of you can compromise, because your values are essential to who you are. *When you have widely differing values, you may not be able to create or maintain a solid relationship. You may have to let it go, because staying means continuing in a relationship that's conflicted to the core.*

Yes, some couples who share vastly different values *do* make it—but only because they are exceptional communicators, maintain a very high level of respect for the other person's beliefs, like each other a lot, and are able to compromise. Unless you and your partner share those traits on a regular basis, you will face a lifelong (and likely futile) struggle to reconcile your contrasting values.

Following are some of the core values a person may have that aren't likely to change.

Work Life

You or your mate may be defined by work, making it a core value. Some elderly individuals, still working long past retirement age, feel that work gives them a reason to keep going, maybe even more than relationships. Work is often valued for all the mental, emotional, and physical benefits of being *productive*. Or, you may value the position and prestige that comes with your work. You don't have to be a great surgeon or hold a high public office to have work with prestige. Some less publicly exalted jobs bring big social rewards. If one of you values your job in this way, nothing is likely to change it—not getting married, nor having children, nor relocating.

Money

The value you or your partner place on work may be tied to the money it earns you (or him). Some people would do their jobs whether or not they got paid, but that isn't true for most people. Money earned through effort is an important measure of status and significance. Some folks feel their salary is a reflection of how important they are in the workplace. This can motivate achievement-seeking at work and keep individuals focused on their jobs.

There are cultures and subcultures who value *not* working, however. You may feel a higher prestige in having someone else support you. In the past, men worked so their wives were able to stay home. A wife who didn't work was a measure of a man's success and financial status, but that is no longer a central societal value. At this time there is more focus on men being able to be home more to help raise children. This aspect of work is a value that straddles both the child-rearing area and the income area.

Some people place significant value on being able to make money. Money means success, and success can be seen as a reflection of an individual's capability: his or her worth as a person. Cash can seem to confer power to a person, and in some ways, this is clearly true. You have the power to buy things, to be independent.

It isn't important to some, however, to spend all their time chasing the buck. If their bills are paid and they can afford a roof over their heads, they're all set. Some people feel their contributions to the social fabric of their communities or the time spent raising children is more important than income.

Faith's Story:

I never realized when we got together how big this thing was about Craig coming from a family with a lot of money. My mom and dad did okay, but we kids always knew there was a budget and we didn't get everything we wanted. We were okay with that. I was raised with the understanding that I had to pay my own way through college, and I worked hard to get scholarships. I worked a part-time job and I'm still paying off some school loans, but I feel good about having made my own way. It never occurred to me that Craig not having had the same experience would be a problem.

We were both sophomores when we met at a party. I thought he was cute, but I knew he dated a lot and pretty much slept with everyone. I resisted him when he wanted to go out with me. I didn't need to be another notch on his bedpost. After a while, though, he got through to me that he was serious about wanting to see me. We dated for more than a year and didn't get married until we'd been out of school a year and a half.

I guess the big problems didn't become clear to me until a couple of years after that. I mean, Craig and I were just getting used to being married in the first few years—that's what I'd tell myself. When he quit his third job, though, I got really upset. He didn't think it was any big deal. When I talked about paying the bills, he said he'd get money out of his trust fund if he needed to. I wasn't comfortable with that, but I didn't know how to tell him he couldn't. After all, it's his money.

Even though this bothers me, he doesn't work consistently. He owned a nightclub for a while and then sold it. He's been building an alternative-fuel car with a friend of his now, but he doesn't go in to the shop every day. They both seem to feel really casual about their goal.

This has gotten to be a big issue for us, though. I've worked several jobs at a time to pay the bills. I feel strongly about paying my own way. Craig doesn't seem to care. While I've always put a high priority on being a good employee, Craig just dials it in. He really just doesn't seem to care about having a career or doing anything, really.

When our son was born, we were both thrilled. I guess I thought Craig's "provider" gene would kick in then, but nothing really changed. I have my own business now and I work hard juggling everything, but Craig just quit another job. This time he just didn't like the people he was working with. I'm pulling my hair out. It just doesn't seem to matter to him. He's not working now and he spends most of his time playing golf and goofing around with our son. He takes care of the baby when I'm working, but he's just floating along, sucking off his inheritance.

I've tried telling him that this isn't a very attractive thing to me, but he doesn't get it. He says why should he work when he doesn't have to? I guess—for me—work has always been a part of who I am, and I'm not sure who he is anymore. This is getting to be a real problem between us.

The problems between Faith and Craig come from them having different values about money and work. If Craig doesn't recognize that this is a major issue for Faith, she'll continue to be frustrated and gradually become disenchanted with the relationship. Faith doesn't see Craig's contributions to the family—she doesn't value his caring for their son—because he doesn't work outside the home. She needs to see that although he may not provide for the family in the traditional sense, he does give a significant amount in assuming the caregiver role. If this is threatening to her or she wants to be the caregiver, while he provides a living for the family, she needs to talk about this with Craig. They could take turns in this role or assume a fifty-fifty parenting model with both of them earning money and sharing the caregiving for their child.

However they choose to resolve these conflicts, Faith and Craig need to come to terms with their different views of these issues. Conflicting values strike at the core of relationships.

Having money is generally seen as a good thing. Most people
would like to have a trust fund, even if they don't identify a high
income as a strong value. Money enables individuals to pursue certain options that they otherwise couldn't. Some things are certainly
easier if one is well off. But, as you can see from Faith and Craig's
situation, money doesn't automatically convey happiness. There are
many incidences in the media of individuals who have a big income,
but poor quality of life.

Education

For some individuals, education is an important value. You may
come from a background that values higher education—bachelor's,
master's, and doctoral degrees—if members of your family attained
them. Other families strongly value academic performance through
high school, but think college—or graduate work—is unnecessary.

Having Different Personalities

Couples often conclude, after running into a relationship wall over
and over, that they're too different and can't resolve to build a life
together.

Maybe. Maybe not.

Having different values, as just discussed, can mean you don't
have a foundation on which to build a relationship. If you're differ-

ent *on a personality level*, though, that's another ball game. If one of you is significantly more outgoing than the other or if one is more visible with his or her emotions, you can offer each other a good counterbalance. But some couples in this situation think "we're just different people" and that they can't reconcile their contrasting personality styles.

It's Important to Have Different Personalities
There's no such thing as a conflict-free relationship. It's okay if you and your partner have different personalities, but make sure that your differences balance out one another.

In a lot of ways, it's healthy and fun to have a personality different from your partner's. It's like playing on a seesaw—you have more fun if someone is sitting opposite you. You might prefer to have everything planned, but your mate might like to fly by the seat of his pants, planning nothing. Both of these can be personality strengths. Planners need spontaneity to keep from going stale. Spontaneous folk need to have enough structure to get the bills paid on time. There's a place for both. Relationships between individuals who are too similar often lack excitement and passion.

ASK YOURSELF:
1. Do I prefer to always know what's ahead, or can surprises sometimes be fun?
2. Am I comfortable with big groups of people, or do I like to have one or two really good friends?
3. Can people pretty much tell what I'm feeling from my facial expressions, or do I prefer to keep my emotional cards close to my chest?
4. Do I like to take risks and try new, unusual things, or am I more comfortable with the things I'm used to?

These questions help identify aspects of how you see yourself and the world around you. Your personality was formed early in life, and it's important to appreciate who you are. This can be harder when you're in a relationship with someone who is very different from you. Individuals tend to think their way of seeing the world is the only way to look at it! Of course, that's not true. Being able to consider other people's lives and worldviews and accept that it's okay to be different is a sign of personal maturity. Learning new ways of looking at situations can open up your own awareness. Even if you don't change your view of things, you can benefit from seeing the value in another point of view.

Social Life

One of the biggest personality conflicts couples deal with is how much social life they prefer. Some people love being surrounded by friends and family. They even enjoy talking to strangers and chat easily with them. Being totally alone for any period of time may be uncomfortable for these extroverts.

On the other hand, more introverted individuals need time alone to recharge their batteries. This doesn't mean they're antisocial or that they don't like people. They just don't always want a crowd.

These two people can offer one another balance *if* they learn to respect and value each other's perspective. The difference between making it and not making it as a couple can come down to that "if."

How to Make Different Personalities Work Together

Personality differences make things more interesting and challenge you to be a more complete person. This is not to say they're always fun; having different personalities leads to conflicts, but these are *workable conflicts*. Sometimes, you may feel misunderstood. Sometimes you may not understand how he can see things a certain way, when it seems so bizarre to you.

Remember, you can't change his personality. Believe it or not, you wouldn't want to. Every type of personality has its own gift. He can adjust and adapt to your perspective, and you to his, but seeing everything the same isn't even something you want.

Don't think life would be easier if you were with someone who's more similar to you in personality. This isn't a solution. It's like being in a relationship with yourself. You may feel *soooo* understood at first. It may seem that he gets you in a way few others have, but after a while, personality similarities leave you unable to resolve conflicts.

If your personalities are very similar, you probably have similar skill sets. You may both feel bad about the conflicts and not understand why you keep struggling with these things. You may wish you could get along, but you won't have even the beginnings of the tools needed to work out problems. The two of you might eventually bore the heck out of one another, and you may find yourself attracted to some other guy.

When He's *Done* with You

Just as you can't change your partner's values or his personality, neither can you change his mind if he's decided to leave the relationship. If he's made a decision to move on, you'll need to accept it—as sad, overwhelming, and life-altering as that is. You may instinctively try to change his mind, but you can't.

Here's what *not* to do if you get the news that your partner wants to end your relationship:

- Don't call his mother or his best friend, crying about him. Their loyalty isn't to you.
- Be careful of pouring your heart out to your friends. They probably struggle with relationships, too, and if you do get back with him at some point, he won't want to be around them.

- Don't put your life on hold indefinitely to wait for him. Go on living.
- Don't start dating other men simply because you hope he'll get jealous and want you back.

This probably seems really, incredibly unfair. Just because he's having some problems, *he* gets to decide for the both of you? You guys had a life together. What if *you* want to work this out? You may see lots of possibilities for fixing the relationship. You may suddenly realize that you need to bitch at him less or you may think he just needs to *get a job!* Then, you guys won't have problems and you'll be happy like you used to be.

Be Wary of Mind-Changers

If he seems to change his mind about leaving, "listen" to his behavior. Even if he does move back home, it doesn't mean he'll stay there or be emotionally invested in the relationship with you. He might feel guilty—which leads him to move back, but won't ultimately change how he feels long-term about the relationship. Look at *all* of his behavior, not just the bits and pieces that seem reassuring. If he's not emotionally investing in being with you—sorting through the problems and being happy together—you don't really want him back.

Doesn't he owe you this? Maybe it seems like he's throwing away all the love you had and the time you invested. Accepting that he's through just may seem impossible.

Is There Someone Else?

When they get to this place in a breakup, lots of people want to believe their partner has found someone else. And there may very well be someone else, but believe it or not, the other person's not the big issue here. Your relationship with your partner is the issue. You may want to believe that he's been lured by some witchy woman and is being duped into falling in love with her. She may seem like the devil, and you find yourself leaving dirty phone messages for her in the middle of the night or calling her boss to let him know what kind of woman he's employing.

You're forgetting, though, that she isn't the person who owes you fidelity. She's not the one who's been in an intimate relationship with you . . . unless he fell for your best friend. In that case, you've been betrayed twice (which would be the worst of the worst).

Still, the most important issue is his commitment, or lack of commitment—not the other person.

Let It Go

Breakups are rarely clear and clean. With so much of your heart and your obligation to that person tangled up with what your friends and family say (or will say), this situation isn't simple to deal with. If your partner is saying he's finished with the relationship, you may find yourself wanting to call his mother, his brother, or his clergyman.

As I said earlier, that isn't the best idea. When you're trying desperately to hang on to a relationship, it probably seems that you have to use every tool in your tool belt. You might hope he'll listen to these folks, since it probably feels like he's not listening to you. You might be hurt and angry. It's natural to want to lash out when you feel rejected.

 Say This to Him

"I really want this to work out . . . but only if we can both be happy together. Tell me what you've been saying, but I haven't been hearing."

Sometimes, though, you just need to accept it, even though it seems so wrong. He gets to walk away, if he wants to. The hardest part of this can be when he wants to *stay friends* (another term for *torture you*) or if he waffles back and forth. You may think you see in his eyes that he *really wants* to move home and stay with you.

Meg's Story:

Both Isaiah and I were working toward our MBA when we first met. We got to know each other when our instructor assigned us to a group project. We ended up starting to go out and after that, we just hit it off. Within six months we were madly in love and living together. Eventually, we both graduated and got better jobs. It was a good time to make a financial plunge, so we bought a house together and we adopted a pair of raggedy dogs.

We went about our lives and I was happy. I thought he was happy, too. Sure, we had arguments, but we always kissed and made up. The arguments didn't seem to last a long time or leave scars. At least, I didn't think so.

I knew Isaiah didn't like us fighting and, every once in a while, he just gave in to get the argument over. I was cool with this, because I didn't like arguing, either. Sometimes I just decided to let things go, too. It's not necessary fight over every little thing.

Then, Isaiah got a good job in a nearby city. When he was gone a lot, I was okay with it because this was for our future. It was a complicated time for us because I started to get involved with local politics, but Isaiah couldn't always get away to go to meetings and fundraisers with me. I knew he wasn't as interested as I was in all this, but local government was important to me—Isaiah agreed with me about this.

Eventually, it seemed like the more he invested himself in his work, the more I found to do in the political arena. Then one day, almost by accident, I was looking at the cell phone bill—I always like to look at those things to make sure I'm not getting overcharged—

and I noticed one number popping up a lot. It had the same area code as the city he worked in and I just thought it was natural that, in the way of business, he'd talk to people near there. But some calls were at odd times, like on the weekends or in the middle of the night. My first thought was that the cell company made a mistake. I couldn't think why he was talking to whoever this was for an hour after I'd gone to sleep.

When I thought about it, I realized Isaiah seemed more and more . . . distant. I decided to talk to him about this. I guess I hoped he'd have a simple explanation and that we'd laugh about it. But when I talked to him, Isaiah admitted everything. He said he'd fallen in love with a woman at work. He was very straightforward about it, almost like he was relieved.

I was stunned. He moved out that night and took all his clothes. He said he'd be back to get the furniture. I couldn't believe it. I thought we were happy. After he moved out, he started calling me nearly every day. Sometimes, he just wanted to ask how the dogs were doing. Sometimes, he asked about me. Every now and then, he'd call when he'd had a tiff with his new girlfriend. He said he wanted my "take" on the argument.

We were broken up, but I still loved him. I was just sick about all this and I desperately wanted him back home with me and the dogs. I even met him in a park once, so he could talk about things—stuff with *her*. I'm not proud of it, but we ended up having sex in his car. After that, I began to wonder if this was smart and if it was leading to anything. Somehow, I'd become the other woman.

As hard as it is—and it's really hard—Meg needs to move on with her life, as much for any future with Isaiah as for herself. He needs to see her moving on to realize that he can't have his cake and eat it, too. Only by acting on his stated decision to end their relationship can she give him what he says he wants. Without this,

Isaiah never gets to see the reality of his choices, and Meg keeps getting emotionally pummeled.

Meg needs to move on and create a life for herself, rather than waiting and hoping that Isaiah will see how she's changed and miss her enough to come back. She needs to open up her social world, perhaps by joining a faith organization, going back to school to get a degree she's wanted, or just taking lessons in fun activities, like dancing or gardening. Meg deserves better than the limbo she's in now.

Recognize Your Positive Steps

Though we've all heard the adage "opposites attract," this only really works when your *personalities* are opposite, not your values. If you and your partner disagree about several core values, the differences may be too much for your relationship to bear. Accepting this fact is an important and courageous step toward making an informed decision about whether to stay or go. You're making progress if you have identified the things you can't change about your partner that bother you. Once you've done that, decide whether or not those things are deal breakers for your happiness in the relationship. Your happiness is most important—take care of yourself. Soul-searching at this level is extremely difficult, so take pride in your progress thus far.

If he's decided to end the relationship, you can't change that either. The best thing you can do is let him go. It's not the easiest thing, but it's the healthiest option. You're making progress if you can begin to envision a life completely separate from his.

- **You should stay if:** The two of you share a similar value system and you can see how to improve your understanding of one another.
- **You should leave if:** You have key differences in your value system and the only way to make this work is for one of you to demand values changes from the other. That won't happen.

Exercises and Affirmations

Since you've spent a lot of time in this chapter thinking about the negative aspects of your differences, take a moment to think about the benefits your differences bring your relationship. For example, perhaps you are a planner but you actually like his spontaneity (once in a while). Or maybe he is shy, but he likes that you are outgoing so you can help him ease into conversations at parties. These advantages are important, and you should weigh them just as you do the disadvantages.

chapter nine

How to Make Your Relationship Better

Things to Consider

- Are you harping at him all the time?
- Are you so busy trying to make sure he hears you that you don't really hear him?
- Have you given this relationship all you can? It's okay to acknowledge that some relationships can't be fixed.

This chapter teaches you several ways to try to improve your relationship if you've decided to stay. None of the techniques are 100 percent *guaranteed* to work, of course—but they give you and your partner a good chance at learning from past mistakes and building a solid future. Reconnecting with your partner is a difficult process, and things may even seem to get a little worse before they get better. But if you've made your decision and love your partner, you might still have the desire to give this one more shot. Reminding yourself of your self-worth (see Chapter 6) and why you originally fell in love with your partner (see Chapter 7) can help make the process a bit easier.

Learn How to Take Criticism

Knowing your strengths and your limitations enables you to make better decisions and to generally deal with life—and your relationship —better. One of the decisions you'll need to make is how you're going to take criticism. At this point in your relationship, you've probably heard your partner say a lot of not-so-nice things about you. How have you responded in these situations? If you're like most people, you get defensive and immediately feel like you need to explain yourself—perhaps to say he's flat-out wrong or that his actions caused the problem in the first place. While this reaction is understandable, it's not the most effective one. Let's look at how Tiffany decided to hear her husband's criticism.

Tiffany's Story:

When Kyle said he wasn't happy in our relationship, I just panicked. I can see all my flaws. I know I'm a mess. I'm not always happy, either. In fact, I haven't been happy for quite a while now, but I still love him. I'd still like to make this work. I just don't know where to start.

When we went to see the marriage counselor—the one that I found, even though Kyle's the one who's been saying we needed it—I tried to really say what was bothering me. That's what you're supposed to do, right? Really talk about the problems. But Kyle just kept saying, "See? See what I put up with?" I put up with a lot, too. I don't think it's too much to ask that he listen to what I don't like.

I really love him and I don't want a divorce. I grew up in a divorced family and I don't want that for my kids, but he's just not listening. I know he doesn't like things I do, but I don't think he sees that he's kind of making me do the things I do! He wants me to keep the kitchen cleaner and I've tried to do that, but he just says that I don't try. I do try, but we've got kids. I just can't keep everything clean enough and I just can't understand him and, to hear him talk about it, I just suck.

He hardly ever talks about what's bothering him—other than the kitchen floor—and when he does talk about something, I listen. I really do, and then I try to explain to him why I do whatever. He just huffs off, saying that I don't care what he says, but I do.

Tiffany is struggling to listen without being defensive when Kyle tells her what he doesn't like. Defending yourself is a natural inclination, but in this case it doesn't convey that she's really listening. She needs to realize that Kyle's feelings are just that—his experience. She needs to listen to his experience, not react like she's a bad person if she acknowledges his experience. To make this marriage work, Kyle will also have to see that he's contributing to the problems. He needs to talk about what's bothering him, not just what Tiffany's doing wrong. Both need to listen to one another.

Quiz: Are You Condemning Yourself?

On a scale of one to five (with one meaning you disagree strongly and five meaning you agree strongly), answer the following questions:

1. I get angry with him when he talks. _____
2. He doesn't talk about our problems. _____
3. I feel I must defend or explain myself. _____
4. I think I make more bad choices than most people.
   _____
5. I feel like he's telling me I caused most all the problems.
   _____

If you scored 20 or more points: Serious self-image problems are making change very difficult for you.

If you scored 11–19 points: You are struggling with hearing his experience without taking responsibility for what he feels.

If you scored 5–10 points: While you sometimes have a hard time with what he's saying, you usually feel like he's trying to understand.

How to Listen Without Being Defensive

If you feel the need to defend yourself before your partner has even finished talking, it's time to slow down and practice more thoughtful listening. Yes, it can be immensely frustrating to bite your tongue while someone is berating you. But in the long run, your restraint:

- Helps defuse the situation (or at least prevents it from escalating further)
- Prevents you from mishearing or assuming anything (which might happen if you're thinking of a response instead of actually listening, or if you interrupt him before he's finished)
- Shows your partner that you are truly listening and care what he has to say
- Gives you some time to decide how to proceed

  Try this technique the next time the situation occurs:

1. Resist the urge to interrupt and defend yourself. Listen—without saying anything—to everything he says.
2. Take a deep breath and use the listen-and-repeat method (see the next section). Make sure you understand exactly what he's saying. This may require several attempts on his part to clarify what he really means.
3. After you've understood what he's saying, calmly describe the situation from your perspective. Acknowledge your mistakes if necessary (remember, *everyone* makes them, and they do *not* make you a bad person). If the two of you are still talking

without yelling and he seems to be listening, explain anything you think he may not have realized. Then ask him to practice the listen-and-repeat technique so you are sure he understands your point of view.

This way of communicating is a much more productive and loving way to give and receive criticism. It also works to help you reach an appreciation of one another's points of view. If you're going to fix this, you need to understand each other even when you see things very differently.

Communicate More Effectively

People in troubled relationships often struggle with productive communication. You both probably feel that you communicate "better" than the other person. Communication is a two-way street, however. It's important that you both listen and talk. Doing one without the other doesn't work.

Remember the Listen-and-Repeat Technique

As we discussed in Chapter 3, you need to actually hear what he's trying to tell you—even if it's hard to listen to, even if he struggles to tell you what he's feeling. Practicing the listen-and-repeat technique explained in that chapter is a significant part of good communication. Way too often, individuals hear something very different from what their partners intended to communicate.

Reflect His Emotions

In addition, listen to how he feels, not just what he's saying. Is he hesitant to get to the heart of the matter? Does he struggle with anything that seems like conflict because he thinks it never leads to anything good? It's also possible that he might not feel "safe" enough to talk to you because of how you typically respond to him. As you listen, remember that nothing's all your fault (you aren't that powerful). It may seem that your mate thinks everything is your fault, but if you hear his *emotion*, you may find that's not the case.

Start Doing This

Breathe deeply and remind yourself that the *both of you* in this relationship need to improve. When you think about change, realize that this means both partners.

To be sure you're interpreting his feeling correctly, reflect back what he feels—say, "When that happened, are you saying you felt unloved, sad, and ignored?" Since most guys won't identify with you listing off potential feelings, try saying something like, "Are you saying you felt ignored when this happened?" If you connect on this emotional level—without defending yourself—you can communicate about your problems in a more objective and successful way.

When you reflect his emotions back to him, don't argue that he shouldn't feel that way. He has a right to his own reactions, just as you do. Think of yourself as a receiver. You're *just listening*. You're learning his perspective. The key here is to try to communicate in his language, not convert him to your language.

Speak for Yourself

Remember—You can only feel for yourself. Don't tell him what you think he's doing or how you think he feels.

Explain Your Own Feelings

Hearing *his* feelings is massively important. It is, however, only the first step. You also need to tell him what *you're* feeling. Don't start the sentence with "I feel *that you* . . . " though. That's just another way of telling him what he's doing wrong or that his feelings are wrong. Say what *you* feel: "I feel . . . [mad, sad, lonely, unloved, disappointed]."

Talk Productively

Too often individuals talk in "you . . . " statements. For example, "You always leave all the housework for me!" or "You never tell me when I do something right." When something is said in this way, it's easy for the listener to feel attacked and become defensive. This is a no-win for everyone. Instead, try describing your emotions in relation to the situation. For example, say, "I feel very angry when I'm doing all the housework and you're relaxing on the couch. It's unfair; I want to relax too!" The best way to try to solve the problem is to approach it in a calm way that will foster further communication, not shut it down before it's really begun.

ASK YOURSELF:
1. Do I really try to listen to him?
2. Do I interrupt him when he's talking?
3. If I were to repeat back to him what I hear him saying, would he say I heard him?
4. When something bothers me, do I tell him without yelling?

If you don't want to change your bad habits in this part of your relationship, you're refusing to build the foundation of healthy communication. Without that, your relationship will not have the stable ground it needs to grow.

Now, Figure Out *Why* He Feels the Way He Feels

If you're not judgmental and don't tell him he's wrong to feel the way he feels, the conversation might progress to the point where you get to talk about *why* he feels that way. Humans are basically logical. You have a reason for how you feel, even if the reason is based on faulty logic or mistaken beliefs about others and yourself. You still have a reason.

If you believe you're being attacked, you feel anger or fear. You might feel hurt, depending on who's attacking whom. Emotion is based on what you believe. In fact, it is your *assessment* of a situation that leads—in a direct path—to how you feel about it.

So, the *why* is really, really important. It is the belief your partner holds about the relationship, about the situation, about himself and you. You may not agree with how he sees it. In fact, you probably won't agree. This doesn't mean one of you is wrong; it just means you see things differently.

Sometimes, getting to the *why* actually helps ease the entire conflict. *If you understand why he feels the way he does, you realize he's not just trying to give you a hard time.*

You feel differently about him because you feel less attacked, because you see his perspective, because you *understand*. In the vast majority of relationship conflicts, your partner's actions or choices are not meant to harm you. If he loved you enough to be in this relationship, he's *probably not trying hurt you.*

Act Like He Matters

Typically, people do this at the beginning—and the end—of relationships. In the middle, though, most of us do a terrible job at functioning like the person who matters most, actually matters the most.

This isn't because you're stupid or deeply dysfunctional or inherently bad at relationships. When you have someone connected to you intimately, the loved one becomes integrated into you, almost to the point of becoming part of you. You start applying the same expectations to him that you do to yourself. *You start overlooking your partner's needs the way you overlook your own.* On some insensible level—mostly outside your consciousness—you think he knows you love him; he should understand that.

Avoid Coasting

You might have fallen into the trap of thinking *this relationship is forever.* While the concept of constant, enduring love is powerful and very attractive, it's also dangerous. When you think you'll be with this other person forever—that your mate will always love you—you feel warm and secure. You also start to coast. In relationships, you both need to act—every day—like this is the person you want to be with. This person is your highest priority.

You might have children and they, of course, get the highest priority spot when they're young—but don't forget that your primary relationship is the foundation of their home. You and your mate provide the kids with security . . . or not. How this relationship goes is very important to them.

This doesn't mean you don't disagree or that he doesn't sometimes frustrate the heck out of you. It's a reality that in relationships your partner can make you madder than anyone else, but don't think you'll resolve the issue later rather than handling it now. When you frequently back-burner a relationship, you risk losing the relationship itself.

How to Show Your Partner He Matters

If your partner is highly important to you, you take his calls. You take his preferences into account. You listen to his words when he gripes, not just the fact that he's complaining.

Ask yourself whether you know your partner's needs and preferences. Have you considered what he wants from this relationship? Act like he matters.

If you can't make yourself do this, maybe he doesn't matter that much to you.

Know That Sometimes, You Can't Make It Better

This is not fun, but it's sometimes a *reality*: You can't always make the relationship work, no matter how much you wish you could; no matter how hard you try.

If your mate is firmly lodged in the belief that all this is your problem and that he's perfectly fine, *you're probably not going to be able to make this work*. If he believes he hasn't done *any*thing wrong, he's not likely to be concerned with what's troubling you. If he's unresponsive to trying better communication tactics, won't listen to what you're saying, and refuses to approach problems with an open mind, he may have already checked out of this relationship.

If that's the case, it doesn't mean that everything is his fault, either. Yes, some things are his fault—his behavior or non-behavior; his words. These are his choices, his actions. None of this is in your power. You can't make him be a certain way. This isn't in your power and it isn't your fault. His choices are his. He's contributed to how the relationship is currently. He needs to change and meet you halfway, if things are going to get better. But even if he shares the blame, you're not off the hook. You have to change your part, the behaviors you've had that have been damaging to the relationship.

All relationships need to be able to pass the cost-to-benefit test. If this relationship is costing you (meaning you have to give up your career, your family, your position on parenthood) more than it's benefiting you, leaving is the smartest choice. Weigh it out. You won't be happy if you put energy—large amounts of energy—into trying to improve a situation that's not bringing you something valuable. What's your cost-to-benefit ratio? Is this relationship costing you more than it's bringing you? That may be the case if you've tried the ideas in this chapter but don't feel that you and your partner have made any progress.

Recognize Your Positive Steps

Each one of these ideas on how you can improve your relationship is difficult to enact, but each brings its own set of benefits and rewards. You're making progress if you have committed to trying some of these ideas—even when the going is tough; even when you want to fall back into old bad habits. Most important, you may find that the tools for more effective communication help forge a breakthrough that allows you and your partner to connect on a new level.

- **You should stay if:** You're a better person with him than without him.
- **You should leave if:** He doesn't add to your life.

Exercises and Affirmations

Do something fun with friends. This will help you relax and renew, which is hard to do when you're looking at behaviors you have to change. Shake lose some of your stress and have fun with people who like you for who you are. They will help you boost your self-esteem and get rid of self-doubt, which can be overwhelming as you work through relationship troubles. Remember the list of your good qualities that you made in Chapter 6. Be sure you look at that list frequently to remind yourself of your inherent self-worth.

chapter ten

Nine Signs You're Not Finished with the Relationship

Things to Consider

- Are you leaving because others think you should?
- Do you need to change some old behaviors before you can move on?
- Does it feel like you've left the relationship, but you still find yourself pulled back to him in one way or another?
- Is the finality of just walking away freaking you out? Ending a significant relationship naturally leaves you feeling unsettled and at loose ends. You aren't sure what's ahead and whether or not it'll be better. Take a deep, calming breath and remind yourself that you're an intelligent, capable woman, even if you don't feel this way right now. Have some faith in yourself.

Saying you're finished with a relationship is one thing; actually *being* finished is very much another. If you two have fought again and again and you are at the end of your rope, you may swear that you're finished.

But are you?

Some women say they're done and that they're leaving the relationship (sometimes even starting to date others), but aren't actually done. Before you confirm your decision for yourself, consider the signs in this chapter.

While you may want to be finished, you might not be; that's why you're considering staying. If you haven't come to terms with the issues in the relationship, maybe you're not through with it. This chapter outlines some common indicators of whether or not you're truly done. See if anything on this list sets off any warning bells. Exhibiting any of these signs doesn't necessarily mean you *should* stay the relationship—but it means that you're not completely ready to leave it for one reason or another. You may have more to learn or more to accept about what leaving will really mean.

Quiz: Are You *Really* Done?

On a scale of one to five (with one meaning you disagree strongly and five meaning you agree strongly), answer the following questions:

1. You can't envision never having a personal conversation with him again. _____
2. It's important to you to be able to keep him as a friend. _____
3. If certain things were different, you could see yourself getting back together with him in the future. _____
4. You hate his guts and wish he'd suffer forever, with you able to watch. _____
5. You still socialize with him, tell him when he needs to get his teeth cleaned, or call when you have car trouble. _____

If you scored 20 or more points: You are definitely not finished with the relationship.

If you scored 11–19 points: You aren't completely clear on what it means to leave a relationship. You're not fully understanding that if you step out of the connection, you don't get to have input into his life.

If you scored 5–10 points: You are probably finished with the relationship.

Ginger's Story:

My sister keeps saying I'm not over Eric, but she's wrong. We broke up six months ago, but that doesn't mean we don't still care for each other. Eric called me, all upset, when his mother had to go into the hospital. I was there for him, letting him talk about everything. That's what friends do. My sister says it's nuts that I keep his dog when he goes out of town or has to work late, but I love Buster, too. And taking care of him is no big deal. Eric just comes over and gets him when he's back or when his schedule changes. People do that with kids. What's the matter with us both loving Buster?

I know I haven't found a new boyfriend yet, but that doesn't mean I'm still hung up on Eric. I know he's with Adele now. It's not that he and I are still dating, but when he's had a fight with Adele, he calls me to get my take on things. After all, who knows him better than me? We were together for nearly two years. I tell him when he's being unreasonable with his new girlfriend or when he's right.

My sister just about had a cow when she found out that Eric sometimes crashes on my couch. Sometimes, he comes in late from work to get Buster and he falls asleep before he can get up and get home. Sometimes, he and Adele are fighting and he just stays here. It's cheaper than getting a motel room, and their fights usually blow over pretty quick. It's not like I have a boyfriend to get all uptight about Eric being here. I don't see the problem.

I guess my sister thinks I should be like her and her ex-husband. They have a hard time speaking, even when they need to for their son's sake. Eric and I aren't like that. He's an okay guy. We just couldn't make it as a couple. That's all. We're good friends now. I can call him when my car won't start or if I need him to take me to work.

Even though Sis thinks I should be upset that Eric doesn't always tell Adele when he's helping me or when he leaves Buster here, I think that's his problem. What he does with Adele isn't my business and I don't stick my nose into places I shouldn't be. If he wants to talk to me about Adele, he does. Otherwise, I don't ask any questions.

Exes shouldn't put forth energy to become enemies, but Ginger is way overly involved with Eric. She relies on him as if he's still her boyfriend, even though he's dating someone else. He does the same thing with Ginger. As her sister points out, Ginger doesn't have anyone else in her life. Eric's filling all her emotional needs. If she really wants this relationship not to be her romantic life anymore, she needs to put some serious distance between herself and her former boyfriend. Any attempt to be "friends" when a relationship is over usually conceals the difficulty an individual is having with letting go. The fact that Eric's current girlfriend is unhappy with him seeing Ginger, and he's lying about their involvement, are signs that the two of them haven't truly ended their relationship. Ginger needs to stop calling Eric, get a new pet, find new friends to talk to about her day, and start looking at her reluctance to date. Having Eric crash on her couch and talk to her when he's upset indicates that this relationship has just gone underground.

Sign #1: You *Passionately* Dislike Him

This sign may seem confusing—passionately disliking him is a sign that you're *not* done with the relationship? That's right. Why?

The degree of your reaction shows that you're still emotionally entangled. You might feel there are things left unsaid or actions left undone. Since the relationship is so damaged or flawed that you decided to end it, you probably feel frustrated and upset. If you're also fantasizing about going postal on him—yelling, screaming, and so on—you're probably not through with this relationship. It's natural to imagine telling him off. After all, this was the guy you dreamed about living with the rest of your life and now you're having serious problems that you're not sure you can fix.

> **Vulnerability**
> When you love someone, that gives him access to your feelings—you can feel hurt by him. Love involves vulnerability. Broken love hurts big.

If You Imagine Being Physically Violent

To go a step further—if you imagine hurting your partner, it's also a strong indication that you may not be finished with the relationship. Anger is an indicator of emotional involvement. The desire to hurt stems from feeling hurt. (Happy people don't resort to violence.) You're more likely to want to pummel him if you feel that he's hurt you. If he has the power now to hurt you, he still has power in your life. You still hurt, and that pain is linked to this relationship.

A Reaction = A Connection

If you don't see any resolution but you continue to fight, it probably seems like you *ought* to be finished with the relationship. Living in this kind of uncertainty can be hell. You can even come to the place where you want to be finished, just to make it go away and let you get on with your life.

But . . . the hurt you feel can equal an emotional connection to your partner—one you might want to keep working on to fix.

Start Doing This

Let yourself feel angry and hurt and mad. All this makes sense when a relationship ends, but don't confuse feelings with actions. You can hate him, but don't set his car on fire.

The people you love have a special power. They have the access code to your heart. If you care, you've given access to yourself. This kind of vulnerability can manifest as anger. Some people have very violent dreams or thoughts about the man they're leaving. Anger is involvement and connection. If you're still really, really mad at him, you're still connected.

If You Were Ready, You'd Feel Grief

If you've realized this relationship isn't going to work, you're probably feeling grief. You may want to walk away and wish very hard that he'd evaporate. The pain you feel may be due to the end of this relationship. Emotional separation is painful, even if it's also a relief. You once loved him, and it takes a while to sever that emotional connection.

For some people, sadness and loss are more easily borne if they are transformed into anger. Being mad can seem like an antidote for some individuals.

If you once loved him—were *in love* with him—the end of the relationship will be very sad. It's okay to grieve. It's even understandable if you still care for him. If you don't harbor bitterness, you might actually wish him the best. You might even have uttered the complicated "friends" word.

Sign #2: You Call Him "Hon" (or any variation)

It may just be habit, but have you called your partner by an affectionate pet name recently? That's an indication that you're not finished here.

Even a sarcastic use of affectionate terms shows a *connected, involved* pattern of speech. If the two of you have been in conflict a while, using a pet name may seem insignificant—especially if you do it without thinking or in the middle of an argument.

> ### Seeking a Response from Him?
> If you're trying to get a reaction from him, you're still emotionally involved.

You might also sometimes call your mate by a pet name in an angry tone of voice, with the conscious intent to hurt. It may seem ironic and even mean. But if you're trying to remind him of how much you once loved him and how lovingly you've spoken to him in the past, you're still engaged in this relationship. You're attempting to make an impact, to get a response from him. That's connection.

ASK YOURSELF:
1. Can I imagine never talking to him? Ever?
2. Do I have imaginary conversations, saying all the things I'd like to tell him?
3. Can he still make me madder than most anyone else?
4. Am I furious with him?

Quinn's Story:
Ty and I've been having trouble for several years. I've tried to stick it out. I didn't act mad when he was out of work for six months and wasn't even applying for jobs or going on interviews. I was nice

to him when his favorite uncle died and I tried to understand when he shut himself off and went out by himself a lot. After all, he's been through some tough times with me.

But he doesn't seem to be trying to work on our communication and I don't feel like he was interested in me, at all, or concerned about my feelings. It went on like that for months, like we were roommates, or something. Then, when he didn't show up to my sister's wedding, I just had had enough. I'd told him how important this was to her and to me and he couldn't bother to show up for a couple of hours. He didn't even have a real excuse. He just said one of his guy friends needed his help to move! I was so mad I moved out. It seemed pretty clear that I didn't mean anything to him.

Ty acted angry and upset when I left. Every now and then he called me, and sometimes he asked my advice like when we were living together. We got together a few times and did things like go to a movie or eat. He'd tell me he missed me and that he hated our separation. Every once in a while, he came over to my place and we had sex.

I didn't tell anyone that I still saw him sometimes. I really didn't know why I was still sleeping with him. I let my girlfriends and my mother think we were still broken up, and we *were*. I mean, it wasn't like dating. But when he called me one day and I suddenly heard myself call him "baby"—that hit me even harder than having sex with him, and that was when I asked myself if I'd really broken up with him or just moved to a new mailing address.

Quinn and Ty aren't dealing with the conflicts in their relationship, and yet they don't want to move on. They each need to look seriously at what they've contributed to this relationship and work toward changing it. The situation will grow sadder and sadder if they can't make a commitment to resolving the conflicts.

If neither one wants to change the way they've interacted when they were openly in the relationship, the relationship has no chance.

They need to stop seeing one another and to invest in other relationships. Even when they feel sad and have the urge to talk to the other person, they need to make a choice not to fall back on old habits. Neither one actually wants to be each other's *old habit*. They need to change this relationship or really end things.

Sign #3: You're Still Having Sex with Him

There's certainly nothing wrong with having a healthy appetite for sex, but sex with someone you're thinking about leaving is complicated. Troubled couples who continue to interact sexually often claimed this is just about the physical aspects of sexual release. Sometimes, they even say they're having sex with their soon-to-be former mate because—should they leave—they're concerned about finding someone who's both disease-free and normal to have sex with.

You know him, however. He represents safety and reliability, at least in this area.

> ### *Sex and Emotional Intimacy*
> For most people, sex is tangled up with emotional intimacy. Separating feelings from sexuality is difficult, particularly when you're having sex with someone you've had—and probably still have—feelings for.

Some people actually split up—some even legally divorce—and keep having sex with their ex. There may be exceptions (mostly in movies and on hot television shows), but for most people, sex is about emotional intimacy. Even when individuals meet and have sex at the first hello, most expect fidelity and a relationship of some kind. You can't get emotionally intimate with someone you don't know, but sex usually brings with it a sense of this kind of connection. Most people are looking for an emotional connection made through a physical bond, even if they spend most of their energy in the physical act.

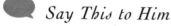

Say This to Him
"We haven't been able — or willing — to fix the prob-lems between us. Until we can do that, I'm not going to keep having sex with you."

For most couples, sexual interaction binds. It brings a sense of connection and, sometimes, a sense of hope—but sex without reso-lution won't fix the relationship. It just keeps the conflict alive and can actually hinder resolution.

Sign #4: You Share "Leftovers"

Some people, after they've broken up, continue contact through shared responsibility to things. Some people have children who still must be parented; they're not the "leftovers." Parenting is very important and, naturally, involves some contact. There are other, less obvious connections, though, and these sometimes indicate a lingering emotional attachment:

- **Storage Units**—Yes, it's true. America is the land of plenty, and we have plenty 'o' stuff. This stuff is packed in basements, garages, and storage sheds. If you've separated from your sig-nificant other but have not fully separated your belongings, this might be an indication that you're not through with the rela-tionship. Are you hanging on to him by hanging on to his stuff in your shed? Or your stuff in *his* shed?
- **Pets**—This is a big one for lots of people. You love your pets, almost as much as your children. (Many people truly think pets are less trouble than kids, and you don't have to send them to

college!) Breaking up often involves having to decide who gets to keep Rocky. Some people determine pet custody by who has the most appropriate housing or who is home with the pet more. Sometimes, though, the pet becomes a really handy way to interact with your former mate. You might find yourself scheduling pet visitation when your former lover has a date or when you know he'll be free to talk (or do other things). Pets can be an excuse for contact. Although it can be heartbreaking, saying goodbye to your partner usually involves one of you also saying goodbye to the pets.

Sign #5: You Haven't Settled the Details

When you're breaking up there are usually a lot of things to work out. If you were married, you've got legal issues. Sometimes, you've changed your name and you have to decide whether to change it back. There also are the financial aspects of dissolving your union.

It's not just cash, either. This might be about more than the goods. While it may seem weird, fighting over the vase you bought together in Europe may be a way to maintain contact. People get passionate about what seem like the smallest things, but those things can be hugely important in the moment. Think about the big divorces and splits that have hit the news. Sometimes, people fight over the smallest, silliest things.

> ## Hashing Out the Details
> Even negative contact is still contact. If you're fighting a battle with your mate, you're still interacting with him.

Maybe the reason you're haggling over details has nothing to do with greed. As long as the two of you are bickering over who gets to keep what, you're still interacting. You still have contact. Fighting can be as intimate as sex. Passion involves risk and emotion.

> **Hanging On for the Wrong Reasons**
> Are you fighting to avoid this relationship being finished? Fighting can seem less painful than having it end, but it's a pain that keeps on giving. Letting go is a pain you pass through and get beyond. If you can't fix this—and only you can determine the relationship's "fix-ability"—you need to move on.

The worst of dealing with the details can be the wrangling over custody of the kids. Individuals can say they are trying to keep their kids safe, but too often this is just an excuse. Arguing over custody may enrich your lawyer but do you and your child harm. If you find yourself unwilling to settle on money or your kids, you may be hanging on emotionally to the relationship you believe you've left.

Sign #6: You're Not Interested in Dating Other People

There are lots of reasons for not dating . . . and one of them is that you're not really through with the relationship. There are some who do "attack dating," which isn't truly an indication of openness to future relationships (think Billy Crystal's character in *When Harry Met Sally*—while Harry is dating other women after his divorce, his then-friend Sally tells him that he's seeing other women and sleeping with them, but not getting emotionally involved).

Jumping from one guy to the next isn't an indication that you're dealing with your grief over the *ended* relationship, either. That's just another way to avoid any true interaction—it's not "real," healthy dating. You're not technically alone, but you're *alone*.

Some people say they're done with relationships after a failed one because they don't want to deal with the challenges that come with intimacy. Some walk away from failed relationships with a sense of having screwed up big time. For them, getting back into another relationship would bring up memories and issues that they don't want to deal with. If you're not sorting through why this one failed—or seems to be failing—you may not be coming to terms with your own emotions. Are you, on some level, pretending that your past partner is just "away" for a while? You might not want to acknowledge that the relationship is over—and that's why you're not ready to date.

> ### Learning from the Relationship
> If you're not learning why this relationship struggled, you might not want to accept that the relationship is over.

Sign #7: You're His Secretary

If you're *really* his secretary, your job's threatened by the very question of whether or not you should leave him. If you don't work together, but you keep his calendar and manage his social or family commitments, you may be more connected than you think. Sometimes, people threaten to leave when there's trouble in the relationship, but they don't mean they're going to end the interaction.

> ### Can You Let Go?
> Keeping track of his calendar is more than a habit. Separation means the two of you living separate—unattached—lives. If you resist that reality, maybe you're not finished.

When it is suggested that they say goodbye and just walk away, these "secretaries" reject the idea as if it makes no sense. Whether claiming to be "friends" (if they really are secretaries) or saying that their husbands/mates need their help to keep functioning, this complete rejection of the suggestion usually means they aren't through. Making his dentist appointments or scheduling when he sees your grown children might be a way for you to stay central in his life.

If you've been with the same man for a while, you may have gotten used to taking care of all the scheduling, correspondence, and so on. However, if you leave the relationship, this role isn't appropriate anymore.

Sign #8: You're Still a Member of His Family

When you're in a committed relationship, you probably have some relationship with members of his family. When you split up, or think about splitting up, this connection changes. When you were actively engaged in the relationship, it probably seemed functional and helpful for you to advise him on how to deal with his mom. If you're still doing this now, however, you might not be finished with the relationship.

Going on extended-family vacations and celebrating birthdays or holidays together after you've decided to split usually indicates ambivalence about ending the relationship. You probably have reasons for participating in these activities. Is it that your mate doesn't want to tell his parents you are splitting and has begged you to "play along" for a while until he finds the right time? If so, why did you agree to this arrangement?

Consider the possibility that you're still performing these roles because you still want to be connected, to be in the relationship.

Sign #9: You Tell Him How to Parent

This is a tough one. After all, the two of you still are parents to the children you share. When you're in a relationship, you get to talk about how the other person parents. Not so, when you're broken up. If you're inserting yourself into his relationship with the children—explaining their father to them or advising him on how to get them to listen to him—you might not be ready to stop sharing your life with his.

This reality has motivated many a couple to reconsider staying in their relationships. The reality of not having a say in how your partner parents can give individuals pause.

Recognize Your Positive Steps

Even though it's difficult and painful at times, you're working hard to be *honest* with yourself, and that's one of the most difficult things to do. If you exhibit the signs discussed in this chapter, the important thing is to learn *why*. If you can come up with a reason for your actions (or inactions), you're making significant progress. Don't beat yourself up for having these feelings; they're normal reactions to the possibility of ending a relationship. Learn from them and you'll be on better footing to make a decision.

- **You should stay if:** You're still tangled up in this relationship and acting connected, even if you're talking about needing to leave. There's more here for you to learn. This may mean you're not ready to leave *yet*, which is also an option.
- **You should leave if:** You can hang on to what you've learned in the relationship, but are ready to fully erase him from your life.

Exercises and Affirmations

First, rent and watch a bunch of sappy relationship movies and cry your eyes out. Watch those in which the relationships work out as well as others in which the characters decide they have to go their own ways. Try *The Way We Were* or *The Break-Up*. Cry. It'll be cathartic, and you'll realize that no matter which decision you make, you can survive.

Second, do something you've always wanted to learn to do, regardless of whether or not you have experience or natural talent at it. This is not about doing it well or racking up a badge; it's about realizing there's a whole world beyond the relationship. If you choose to end it, it's important to begin to integrate yourself into the world outside your relationship.

part iii

if you need to leave

chapter eleven

How to Get an Emotional Divorce

Things to Consider

- Are you very clear that your former relationship is over?
- Can you let yourself feel sad about this loss?
- Can you spend time on just yourself?
- Does the thought of dating someone else excite you or scare you? (Neither emotion means you don't need to date.)

There's no sugarcoating it: Even when you know you need to leave him, actually leaving can be really difficult. How do you just stop caring about him? The answer is that you can't. So even if you're upset and angry with him, acknowledge the parts you loved. They're not enough to keep you in this mess, but *owning up to these moments helps you to feel the sadness of loss, which enables you to move forward.*

This process requires you to separate yourself from him. It's important to think of the two of you as distinct, separate people; you aren't a couple anymore. Think of this as your "emotional divorce." Letting go of the relationship can be both scary and exciting, but moving on requires you to see his life issues as just that: *his.* When you move on without one another, you shoulder the responsibility for your own future, and he for his.

Telling Him You're Through with the Relationship

How you choose to share your news with him is a very individual thing. It's important to be clear and strong in your position, however. This is not the time to "soften the blow" or say that the two of you might get back together at some point. This waffling tone will only give him the impression that the decision *isn't really made* yet. Be kind to him—just tell him this isn't working out and that you're moving on. If you mention how you've reached this decision, make sure you don't slip into defending yourself. There probably isn't a lot to talk about now.

The end hurts; don't let anyone tell you differently. Many emotions accompany this experience: anger, regret, remorse, guilt. It's difficult *not* to feel guilty when a relationship can't be saved. Surrounding these various emotions is usually a deep sense of sadness.

Accept the pain. That doesn't sound fun or fair, but it's what you have to do. Just as when a person dies, you need to let yourself grieve and deal with the loss. You have to go through the soul-searing sadness. Anger. Bargaining. Everything.

Quiz: Have You Accepted that It's Over?

On a scale of one to five (with one meaning you disagree strongly and five meaning you agree strongly), answer the following questions:

1. You're not sure you know why you're leaving. _____
2. Other people tell you that you should stay. _____
3. You frequently wonder how he's doing. _____
4. It seems like you shouldn't be this sad. _____
5. You don't want him completely out of your life. _____

If you scored 20 or more points: You're struggling with the disconnection involved in ending a relationship. This is understandable, but you've got to let go.

If you scored 11–19 points: You're having a hard time making a clean dismount. You've cut some ties, but letting go completely is hard for you.

If you scored 5–10 points: You are moving forward with disconnecting your lives.

Don't Avoid Your Feelings

Some people are so unwilling to deal with their emotions at the end of a relationship—or *feel* so incapable of dealing with them—that they jump straight into a new relationship. At first, a new boyfriend can seem to put several unpleasant feelings to rest. For example, having a new boyfriend may eliminate the fear that you're unlovable and may have to be alone for the first time in (or for the rest of) your life.

Dodging the emotions of grief and fear doesn't really work, however. Feelings find you—in the dark of night or when you're alone or when you get sober. You'll feel the scary emotions at some point. When your emotions start to overwhelm you, take a deep breath and realize this feeling won't last forever. You'll get through the difficult times.

If relationship-hopping is how you *don't deal* with your grief, you'll eventually find it crashing in on you. When it does, you may realize that you've made some bad choices by not dealing with your grief. And don't worry that you might miss Mr. Right. The right guy doesn't usually happen along when you're running from your own emotions. The guy who shows up and jumps in, at that point, is the wrong one.

To truly deal with your feelings, slow down and take a breath. Don't do anything radical. You'll be all right, even if you feel crazed and overwhelmed right now. Don't dive into abusing alcohol or drugs of any kind. You might think numb is better, but numb brings a whole bunch of other problems. Accept that your relationship is over and try to learn from the experience.

> **You Can Do This, Even Though You're Scared**
> You can deal with this breakup. You might not feel like you can do it, but your emotions aren't a complete reality. Just because you feel you're inadequate doesn't mean you are. You can do it.

Be aware that you might get creative in your efforts to dodge your acceptance of your feelings. The avoidance can take shape in a variety of ways—maybe you'll suddenly decide to move to another state, or marry a man you don't know well, or have a baby even though you thought you were finished with child rearing (or have been unsure, up to this point, about the commitments of parenthood).

Know That Things *Will* Get Better

Unlike what you may think at this point, you won't drown in these horrible, ugly emotions. *You won't feel fear and anxiety forever*. Humans aren't made that way. Unless you're constantly re-establishing these negative feelings with your self-talk (things you say to yourself), emotions have a shelf life. They stop in time.

Even the deepest, weeping despair and forlorn grief will lift and you'll begin to feel normal again. Feeling bad—even feeling *really* bad—won't last forever. It's kind of like clouds. They pass, and this will, too.

Don't Be His Friend

Since you've decided that this relationship is over and that you need to move on, *move on*. Don't let yourself think that hanging on to bits and piece of the relationship will make the ending easier. In the long run, it will make everything harder and more painful.

Imagine how keeping him in your life would play out. The idea of him disappearing from your life completely may seem really, really sad, so you try to be friends. You two might not have made it as a couple, but you can surely be friends, right?

No, not really.

> ### Accept That While You May Still Love Him, He's Not Your Friend
> It may be really hard to let go, but hanging on makes it very difficult to move on emotionally. Just rip off the Band-Aid. Goodbye means goodbye. Accept this and be realistic. If being together didn't work out, being *kind of* together won't either.

Friends may have more distance than couples (who typically share a bed, money, and possibly kids), but friends are still affected by one another. If you and this guy couldn't work out an intimate relationship, what makes you think he'll be a good friend? If the two of you were good at working through problems and sharing ownership of property, pets, friends, cell phone plans, vacation homes, storage lockers—everything—you'd probably still be a couple.

Realize It's Not All Your Fault

If separation or divorce means "failure" to you, and you struggle to accept failure (which most people do), this entire process is even more challenging. The "D" word is only fun for lawyers, and even then, only when you're not talking about *their* divorce. But the idea that a relationship breakdown is a failure for the individual ignores the basic definition of relationship. Relationships are complicated and involve two people. Two individuals decided to engage in this relationship. No matter how you slice it, the interaction in a relationship—either good or bad—can't be one person's failure. Give yourself a break.

It's not all about you.

Start Doing This

Remind yourself that you're among good company. Lots of smart, fun, nice people are divorced or have left relationships, and some of them have left several relationships. Sometimes, you just can't work it out.

Hayley's Story:

My parents are still very much in love, even after thirty-five years. And their brothers and sisters have long, happy marriages, too. Even my cousins are happy in their relationships. I'm the only one who can't seem to make it work with my husband. I've tried, but I just can't make Jake happy.

We're both successful in our careers and we have three wonderful children, but something's missing for him. I'm just not enough.

The first affair was with his office manager. He came and confessed that one to me and I was really relieved and happy that he was giving her up and wanted to stay married to me. That was ten years ago and he recently confessed that he's been seeing other people all this time. He's in love with the woman he's involved with now and he says he doesn't know what to do.

I know I'm intelligent and really good at what I do, but I must be bad at being a wife. I've known for some time that Jake hasn't been happy with our love life. He wants me to be more spontaneous and aggressive. He tells me even now that he's attracted to me and still wants to have sex, but I just freeze up. I love him and I want this to work out, for our children as much as anything else, but I can't seem to loosen up and show him sexually that I still want him. I feel dead inside.

I know Jake's infidelity is bad, but I'm also very aware of my own limitations and the mistakes I've made in the marriage. I know I haven't been very warm with him and I accept what he says about me being emotionally unavailable. I have been shut down. For a long time now, I haven't felt very successful as a woman and that's made it hard for me to let him be close. I just don't know what's the matter with me.

Hayley looks around her at the apparent success of other marriages in her family, and thinks she ought to be able to—all by herself—make hers work. It's important for her to realize she can't be totally responsible for the marriage's problems. Marriage takes effort from both parties and one can't be responsible for the other's infidelity, even if she is less than perfect. Hayley's experiencing both low self-esteem and confusion about what any one person can do to change a relationship. She needs to accept that she's been married to a serial cheater and that her husband made many choices that helped end this marriage. She can't take responsibility for causing him to do this. She has to realize that marriage takes both partners investing in the relationship to work through the issues.

ASK YOURSELF:
1. Am I taking more than my fair share of the responsibility for this relationship ending?
2. Am I trying to hang on to some parts of this relationship, even though I know it's over?
3. Can I let myself experience the grief of this ending?
4. Am I assuming complete responsibility for us not making it?

If you're just looking at your own failure—how you might not have been perfect or are far from perfect—you might want to ask yourself if you did all you could do. This is all that can be expected of you. As callous as it may seem, you aren't at fault for his issues. You can't change them. You can't do one dang thing to make him think or act differently. You only have control over your own actions.

Worry about Yourself

Power can be both seductive and burdensome. Don't take his. Handling your own power—managing your own choices—is hard enough.

You Only Have Power over Yourself

You only have the power to change yourself. If you feel you've failed in your behavior, then you need to do some self-exploration. But you don't get to be responsible for *his* failures. He has that power. Don't rob him of that. Don't try to save him. He needs to do that on his own.

The Relationship Failed, Not You

Learn from what happened in your relationship, but don't assume that you're a failure because of the breakup. Nor should you move ahead trying to make sure you never make a mistake or a bad choice again. Go ahead, live your life. Failure is simply life's way of saying *next time, try it a little to the left*. It's corrective, not condemning.

Dealing with Guilt

Guilt comes in two flavors:

1. The emotion of guilt (legitimate or not)
2. The reality of responsibility for a behavior—or not acting when you should have acted

Looking back, you may realize that there were moments when your behavior was hurtful and not loving. It's important to see the difference between the guilt you've legitimately earned and feelings of guilt that are misplaced.

Deserved Guilt

Okay, you messed up. You weren't the perfect partner. You did something you're not proud of and you are a jerk (or so you tell yourself). "Deserved guilt" can arise if:

- You did something that caused a specific breach in the relationship.
- You cheated. You ran up secret debts. You didn't listen to him. You always expected him to adjust; never you.

This kind of guilt feels really bad and it can consume you if you're not careful. Guilt can make you say *I am a bad person*. But if you stop and wallow in that belief, you'll not only have a really bad week (or longer), you'll also miss out on the lesson this experience can bring you. There's something here for you to learn about your actions. Don't let your feeling of guilt block it.

Life isn't about always doing it right. It's about learning from the messes you make.

Undeserved Guilt

If you haven't done anything seriously wrong, the guilt you feel is probably undeserved. You're not completely responsible for the failure of this relationship. He's certainly made some bad choices, even if yours seem larger to you. He's contributed. He's done—or not done—things that didn't nurture the relationship. It's not all you.

It's very important to challenge the thought that you're just a *bad* person. Relationships are difficult. Really, really difficult. Probably one of the most difficult interactions humans have. Yours didn't fail because you're not as good—or as smart—as you ought to have been. This is just poor logic. You might feel bad—which is very understandable—but don't let yourself believe you're a bad person because you couldn't make this relationship work.

Don't Get Stuck

Whether the guilt you are feeling is deserved or undeserved, it's natural to feel bad—responsible and guilty—when a relationship fails. After all, you put a lot of effort into it. It is very, very important that you don't get stuck in the guilt. Not making mistakes isn't even a possibility for anyone. Instead, *learn something from your mistakes.* It's the gift that every mistake brings you. Ask yourself, How could I have handled things differently? What motivated my self-destructive behavior?

Endless guilt is counterproductive. If you continue to mull over and dwell on all the wrong, bad things you did or what you should have done instead, you waste a tremendous amount of energy. And all that dwelling doesn't gain you anything. You don't feel better and the relationship isn't magically resurrected.

Accept Your Limitations, but Love Yourself Anyway

Every individual has struggles. You're no different in this and, most likely, no better or worse than the next woman. Although you might feel awful about yourself, that emotion springs from the mostly inaccurate things you're telling yourself. Love yourself by challenging this kind of inaccurate thinking. No one is who he or she wants to be *all the time.*

Life is an opportunity to change what you feel needs changing about yourself. However, you have to believe in yourself to access the strength to do this. Believing is logical, not emotional.

Negative self-talk and guilt that you foster and focus on is a kind of backward indulgence. Don't go there. Instead, remind yourself of the list of your best qualities that you made in Chapter 6. You are worthy of love and a second chance.

Recognize Your Positive Steps

You left a situation that wasn't good for you and now you're doing your best to make sure you don't repeat mistakes. That takes guts. You're making progress if you can think about your past mistakes without immediately berating yourself for making them. In addition, if you can identify what you would do differently next time, you're much more likely to make healthy decisions for yourself in future relationships. That's a huge accomplishment—many people spend a lifetime making poor choices because they don't stop to evaluate what they could have done better. When you've reached this point, you are in a healthy enough place to begin dating again.

- **You're not ready to date someone else if:** You're still calling, texting, or phoning your ex and having any conversations not related to shared children. If you keep dwelling on the relationship and thinking about what either one of you could do to fix it, you're not ready for another relationship.
- **You're ready to date someone else if:** You're able to grieve and feel sad about the lost relationship without diving headfirst into another one.

Exercises and Affirmations

Take a day to clean out all your "relationship clutter." You might not be ready (or feel the necessity) to burn the photos and mementos, but you don't need them staring you in the face every day either. Pack it all up and put the box in the attic, storage unit, or the back of the closet. You're moving on. You need to clear some space for your new life.

Give yourself a gift to commemorate the forward progress in your life. This might be as expensive as a good piece of jewelry or may simply be symbolic, like a very nice pair of pajamas that you'll wear now to sleep in by yourself. Go to your favorite store and pick out something *you* like, considering no one else's preferences.

chapter twelve

Dealing with the Social Fallout of Leaving

Things to Consider

- Have you lapsed into relying on his social world instead of building your own?
- Are you resisting letting go of shared activities?
- Can you change your actions to make the next relationship better? Continuing the same way is very comfortable and automatic, but it's not always the right thing to do.

After you decide to end a relationship, you face the challenge of rebuilding a life on your own. This is no easy feat—the longer you have been with your partner, the more your lives have become intertwined. You probably share friends and social groups. You may know and love his family. When should you maintain connections, and when must you let them go? There is no easy answer, but this chapter will help you navigate the social complications that arise post-breakup.

Quiz: How Do You Feel about Building a New Life?

On a scale of one to five (with one meaning you disagree strongly and five meaning you agree strongly), answer the following questions:

1. You're starting a new life and that scares you. _____
2. You're worried about what other people will say about the relationship ending. _____
3. Sometimes you feel excited and almost giddy about this new phase of your life. _____
4. You're worried about how the breakup will affect your friend-ships. _____
5. The breakup feels like a personal failure—sometimes his, sometimes yours. _____

If you scored 20 or more points: Congratulations, you're completely normal. Relationship endings come with uncertainty and fears. This is natural.

If you scored 11–19 points: You've probably known for some time that you needed to separate, as hard as that can be. Getting here is almost a relief, even if you're worried about how it's going to work.

If you scored 5–10 points: You're facing this new phase without a lot of anxiety, but make sure you're in touch with how you feel about this. Denial of emotions isn't healthy.

Who Gets the Friends?

If you have good friends—maybe a couple the two of you have hung out with for years—remember that they're trying to deal with your split, too. If they're close friends, they've probably tried to help you save your relationship. They've offered advice and support. They've probably talked about their own rough patches. You may have stayed over at their home when you left him, or perhaps he's bunking there still.

The First Step: Tell Them

Now that you've made your decision to let go of this relationship, you might be dealing with your friends' continued efforts to help you piece this thing together. After all, if the two of you split, it will have a big effect on them and their social life. Once you've decided to move forward in your life, you'll need to tell them. This can be emotional and awkward, but just do it. Let him tell his closest friends, and you tell yours. This isn't a shared activity. After all, the two of you aren't sharing a life anymore. If you both feel close to the same friend, then you'll each talk to the friend separately.

Remember, the failure of your relationship means several significant things to your friends. They won't be able to hang out with the two of you like they used to, plus they must decide whose "side" they'll be on. You may not have asked this of them, but they'll probably still feel in the middle. They love you both. They've witnessed the difficulties. They've probably been the ones you confided in through this whole mess.

Natalie's Story:

Hayden and I met Meg and Darrell just after we moved to Milwaukee. Darrell and Hayden worked together and we were all about the same age. We had fun together and started hanging out all the time. Our kids, Emily and Jake, were six and eight and liked playing with their kids, too. Meg and I used to gripe about the guys, and she became my best friend.

It wasn't until the problems with Hayden and me got really out of control that I started seeing problems with me and Meg. At first, I'd gripe about Hayden, and Meg acted like she understood. She'd talk about how Darrell made her crazy sometimes, too. We had some real girl talks and, after a particularly bad fight with Hayden, I started calling her when I needed someone to listen. After a while, the marriage just got to be hell and I started thinking about leaving him. I didn't think it was good for Emily and Jake to hear us fighting. One day, Emily even asked me if her dad and I were going to hit each other. That really floored me and, after that, I knew that the situation between Hayden and me was hurting the kids.

I starting thinking about leaving him then, planning it actually. But when I began talking about this, I noticed Meg didn't have much to say. Our phone conversations got shorter and then it seemed like she never called me; I had to be the one to call her. When everything with Hayden and me blew up, I didn't have the time or energy to talk with Meg about our friendship. I did ask her once if Darrell felt like he was in the middle, with Hayden and I divorcing. She quickly answered that he didn't; he'd always been closer to Hayden and he didn't see any need for that to change.

I knew then that Meg was the one who felt in the middle. She's married to Darrell, and his friends are naturally going to be her friends.

It felt strange between she and I then, because I knew I was kind of a problem for her. She and I talked on the phone a couple more times, but I didn't feel like I could open up to her the same way as before. She was classified in my mind as "Hayden's friend" from that point on. I felt sad about that, but it just seemed to be the way things had to be.

Natalie's friend had a choice to make, and maybe because of the way Hayden felt about the divorce or how Darrell and Meg felt, the friendship wasn't ever the same. Divorce between couple friends can be scary and unsettling for the still-married friends. Natalie's friends didn't know how to be with her without choosing her over her ex. It was Darrell and Meg's decision on how they wanted to handle the shift, and Natalie is correct in accepting their decision. Even if she thinks Darrell is pressuring Meg to drop her, it isn't her place to confront Meg about their relationship. Challenging her friend on this topic could leave the impression that because Natalie's chosen to divorce, she wants to cause trouble in Meg's marriage, as well.

Taking Sides?

Even if your relationship split is amicable (lovely word), it may seem like a *Who Gets Who?* contest, in which the two of you fight over the friends. It can be like a custody battle, with less financial cost, but almost as high an emotional cost.

Sometimes friends may have already chosen for themselves; otherwise, you might have found yourself trying to persuade them (especially if you've felt so frustrated that you've talked to them quite a bit about what a jerk he can be). If he's said bad things to you about them, you may not care who they pick. No matter what you or your ex say, your friends will make their own choice—one that you must respect. Just as Natalie did, you need to accept their decision and recognize that it probably wasn't an easy one for them to make.

Keep in mind that your split may also have the side effect of freaking them out. If you two looked really solid (meaning, dysfunction was well hidden), your split-up can leave them gasping. If *you* can't make it, what chance do *they* have? Even if your couple problems were hanging out there for the whole world—including them—to see, they're still going to grieve your breakup. After all, the change in your couple status really does affect them. The whole thing really can be distressing, even if they've had a dozen friends go through it. Even if they've gone through it themselves.

All of this is part of the social fallout when you split up. You are left dealing with it, even if it seems like you're dealing with too much already. You need to do your part in making this better. Don't put your mutual friends under even more stress by asking what your ex is up to. This doesn't make things any easier for you, and it only makes everything more difficult for your friends.

Can You Confide in Your Friends?

How do you talk about your distress with your mutual friends when you know *he's* talking about his side of things with them? Their loyalties are in conflict, even if you've tried (noble of you!) to not make them choose between you.

Start Doing This

Make new friends. Yes, it's difficult, especially in the jumbled time of the changes that come with separation, but do it anyway. Take a class. Join a new church. Learn to square dance. You don't have to give up any old friends who still want a relationship; you just have to prepare for the fact that some friends will go his direction. It's natural. Be ready by expanding your social circle now.

It's very natural for you to have talked with your friends all along about the problems in the relationship. They've probably seen the breakup coming. It's good, though, to keep some of the gory details—the ones you haven't already spilled—to yourself. Remember, they're friends with him, too. Resist the urge to "communicate" with him via what you tell them, assuming they'll pass it on to him. You're done, remember?

You can ease this transition by talking with your friends about the changes and how your relationship with them is different. It's important to tell them how important they are to you and how much you appreciate them being there for you.

Telling Your Parents

For some people, telling their parents about the breakup isn't a big deal, especially if their parents have gone through this with various partners themselves. Then again, it can be harder if your parents have been married a million years. You might be the first one in the family to divorce or never to have married. If they really liked your former partner and thought you might marry him (even if you've never cared about legal ties yourself), your split can be even more jarring for them.

If Your Parents Disliked Him

If your folks disliked your partner, it's probably a lot less difficult to tell them the news. Still, you may feel anxious. Be straightforward and tell them as much detail as you feel they need to know. It's your relationship; you can share as much or as little as you want. Though it may seem cathartic at the moment, try not to let the conversation become a rant about what a jerk he is. You are still grieving the relationship and it can be difficult to hear other people say hurtful things about him, even if you feel the same way.

If Your Parents Liked Him

If your parents loved your partner, it can be very tough to tell them you're breaking up. It can be especially sticky if you've talked your soon-to-be ex-partner into going to recent family gatherings in order to keep your breakup a secret for as long as you could. This was a mistake (which you knew, even if it did seem tempting), but don't dwell on it.

Now is the time to tell your parents you've decided to end the relationship. Don't act as if there is a chance you'll stay together if there isn't. Whatever you do, don't lie. It's too exhausting to keep it up. Even if you have to endure an hour (or a couple of days) of their horrified exclamations, they'll soon grow accustomed to this new reality. They'll adjust, just as you are adjusting.

Remember that this is *your* breakup. You don't need your parents' critique of you regarding what you should have or shouldn't have done. If the conversation is veering this way, change the subject or state simply that this is painful for you to discuss and you don't want to talk about it. You just wanted them to know what was happening.

> **Have Faith**
> Even if your parents love him, they probably love you more . . . and even if they've stayed married forever, they know that relationships are challenging. After all, they've been in one a long time.

If your parents want to "talk" to him—either to give him a piece of their minds or to try to fix the problem—tell them *no*. Be very clear about this. Thank them for caring, but remind them that you're a big girl now (said with a reassuring smile) and that you feel you need to deal with these things on your own. If they still aren't convinced and argue with you about them, pull out the statement that you need them to *believe* in you. You need to know that *they* know you can handle this.

Despite everything you say, they might, in their parental desire for you not to make a mistake you'll really regret, try to talk you into giving the relationship one more shot. This situation can be challenging, but you can address it with confidence because you didn't make this decision lightly. Tell them that. Tell them the relationship has been bad for a long time or that it's very, very bad now. You don't have to justify your decision, but tell them the reality so they understand where you're coming from.

The Calm after the Storm

No matter how they initially handle the news, your parents want you to:

- Be happy
- Feel comfortable talking to them about your problems

- Listen if they have suggestions (you don't have to take them, but do respect the fact that they're trying to help)

You might hesitate to break this news because you don't want to disappoint them. If their reaction to your struggling relationship is to be disappointed in you for not making it work, you probably have other, more complicated parent issues. It's probably not all about the breakup. If that's the case, consider seeking professional help to work through these issues.

ASK YOURSELF:
1. Am I afraid my parents will doubt my decision because *I* doubt myself?
2. Do I want my parents to freak out about the split so I have a reason to go back?
3. Is this just one more thing I'm dreading talking to my parents about because my relationship with them is conflicted?
4. How much of my anticipation of their distress is because I feel like a failure myself?

Losing His Family

Not everyone loves their in-laws, but some people do. If you have a great friendship with his sister or his mom or if you've felt welcomed into this family in a way you don't feel with your own, splitting up can be harder. This family connection can make leaving him even more difficult. You might be wondering how a breakup will change your relationships with his family members.

Face some realities: It'll probably change everything. If they have to, they'll choose him over you. This can be sad and heart-wrenching, but it's just how it works. They're likely biologically related to this man. They raised him from a child. He gets their loyalties.

If he's okay with them staying friendly with you, you might hang on to the relationships with them. This depends on how he feels about you and the breakup and how they feel about what their loyalty to him requires.

Guess Who Wins?

If they have to choose sides—and sadly, they usually do—he'll win most of the time. In the rare instance in which there isn't animosity between a splitting couple, the ex might remain close to the family. This arrangement, however, doesn't happen often. Of course, when you have children together, the rules change. Grandparents may privately take sides, but if their access to your children is threatened, they'll at least treat you civilly. Still, relationship endings can get ugly and, if your children's grandparents have access through the father, they may get ugly with you, too. This new animosity might seem very personal and very upsetting, particularly if you thought you had a close connection previously.

Think of the Bigger Picture

Even if you've lost your own relationship with his parents, consider these principles of smart parenting:

- Kids benefit from having a relationship with grandparents.
- Unless his parents are criminals, foster their involvement in your kids' lives, no matter how mad at him you may be.
- Sometimes, you might need a break. Guess who can baby-sit!

Remember that this situation is probably distressing to your ex, too. His parents may be responding to his pain by treating you coolly.

Chyanne's Story:

Ben's mom, Sue, has always been very supportive of me. Sometimes it seems to me that Sue was harder on Ben than she was on me. When he quits job after job and doesn't come home when he said he would, both his mom and I get angry with him.

Ben's behavior is irresponsible, but he doesn't see it that way. I've talked to him about our future and wanting a house for the kids, but he just says I need to quit blowing things out of proportion and that I shouldn't worry so much. He says things will "work out," but he keeps acting like a teenager. I used to feel sorry for him and think he had really bad luck, but I feel more and more frustrated. I tell his mother I feel like I have three children, instead of two.

His mom is as upset with him as I am. When Ben shows up late for family gatherings and sometimes comes an hour or two after the kids and I get there, his mom is pissed and tells him off right there in front of everyone.

I tried to make our marriage work for ten years, tried to make a life with a man who acted more like a teenager than a responsible father to his two kids. Then, I started wondering if I should leave him. Ben's choices just weren't getting better. If anything, he's more and more like a bad example to our son. I know a boy needs his father, but Ben doesn't seem to even care about that.

The clincher for me came when Ben was arrested for driving under the influence with the kids in the car. I knew then that I had to end the marriage.

To my shock, Ben's parents not only bailed him out of jail, they paid for a lawyer to handle his defense. They let him move home when I kicked him out, and then they paid for another lawyer for him when I filed for divorce! I thought we were in agreement that he needs to grow up, yet here they are still taking care of him.

It's like his mom thinks I'm the enemy now. We used to be able to talk about things, but that's over. The last thing his mom said to me after I filed for divorce was that she was standing up for her son's rights.

He needs to do this for himself, not have his mommy take care of him still!

Chyanne failed to notice that Sue treated Ben like a teenaged boy, despite his physical maturity. Family relationships can be complicated, but don't expect parents to take sides against their son. Chyanne needs to realize that her leaving Ben has changed everything. Since she's walking away from Ben, she's left the "club" she's been in with his mom. It's important to realize that some parents like to tell their kids when they're wrong, but that doesn't mean they won't align with their child when a divorce is happening. Chyanne and Ben's mom no longer have Ben in common.

Hello! These Are His Parents

You might be surprised by how partisan your ex's parents become. They may seem, suddenly, to hate you—even if he's been a far-from-satisfactory son. Try not to take this personally. Yes, I know their comments—usually repeated to you by your ex—might be hurtful. Still, their supposed animosity might not really be about you.

Remember:

- They raised your husband.
- He's likely to be their first priority.
- Don't be spiteful, especially when it comes to giving them access to their grandkids.

If They Speak Ill of You to Your Kids

The situation can get really tense if your in-laws make remarks about you when your children can hear them. Your kids will probably be upset and they may repeat comments they've overheard (or that were actually said in their presence).

Take the high road. You love your kids, no question, but that doesn't make them angels. Kids lie sometimes, or they miss nuances in conversation that adults understand. This is not because they're bad; maybe they just want to stir things up so you and their father will talk. It's also possible that his parents DID say something bad about you. Now is *not* the time to try to straighten out the older folks. Convey to your kids that it's upsetting to have people they love talking negatively about each other. Remind them that their grandparents are probably worried and upset. Do this even if you're steaming mad. Whatever the reason the comments were made, it is important not to allow your kids to get into grown-up conflicts.

Understanding Their Anger

Even if your in-laws were angry when they said something about you that the kids overheard, it's not an excuse. Your in-laws are adults and they need to be aware of the potential impact their words can have. Still, they might slip. They may have spoken in the heat of the moment and be ashamed now of what they said. Unless this is happening chronically, you might want to give them a break. Divorce is difficult for everyone, even those as peripherally involved as grandparents. If there are a few rough weeks or months, let it slide. It'll probably pay off for you in the long run.

 Say This to Yourself
"If he were my son, would I still keep talking badly about him to his ex?"

Though it's extremely difficult, try not to take what they say personally. Why? Consider these facts:

- If this were your son, don't you think you'd be on his side?
- They probably don't play bridge with his other exes, either.

- You won't be happy staying in an unhappy relationship for the sake of in-laws you like. Sometimes, you just need to move on.

It's also important to note that some individuals deal with any conflict by getting mad. In this case, they're going to get mad at you. A certain amount of animosity is typical in this situation. They love their son and their son is hurting, in part, because of actions you're taking. Yes, he was half this relationship and is certainly half of the reason why it's ending—if not more. It doesn't matter; they will still direct the heat at you. They may get mad at him too, but you may or may not hear about it. If his parents deal with most conflicts by getting mad, don't think they'll act any differently in this case.

The Bottom Line: Rejection (by Someone You Cared for) Sucks

You may be the wronged one. You might have turned the other cheek with their son until you couldn't turn any more. You might have been the daughter they never had.

Yet once you decided to divorce their son, it's all different.

It's okay to feel hurt. You loved these people and now they're cold. They may even act like they hate you. Go ahead and feel mad, sad, and frustrated—those are natural reactions to this situation. Grieve your loss. The sadness won't last forever.

Being Single

When you've been part of a couple and you're not anymore, being alone can feel—well, lonely. This is true even if your relationship was deeply conflicted. You're smart enough to know that not all the couples at a restaurant are happy together. You've been there. You've been part of an unhappy couple doing couple things.

At the same time, it can be ironic that all you thought about was what a relief it would be to *not* deal with the crap that came with being with him. You longed for this relief, this solitude. So how come you feel lonely now?

You might find yourself thinking about all the good times with him. When you've split up and you're dealing with the transition to singlehood, all the issues in your relationship can start to seem *not that bad*. After all, even though you're not dealing with constant bickering or a cold war in the home, being alone isn't all good, either. It isn't until your relationship is dissolving that you begin to notice how many couples there are in the world. Families with both a mother and a father. Everyone seems to have a mate, a matching bookend, an *other*. Everyone but you.

Right? Wrong.

The good news: Acute consciousness of singlehood is usually a transitory experience. You'll get over it.

The bad news: Transitions don't usually feel good.

Going from "two" to "one" can be startling and affect so much more of your life than you imagined. Hosts at restaurants ask if you're alone or whether someone will be joining you. Who will go to concerts with you? You might have single friends to hang out with, at times, but you'll buy your groceries alone or with your children. You'll go to museums on the weekend and feel like you're surrounded by couples. Your single state is still a new thing. Naturally, you're going to be hyperaware of it.

Take a deep breath and look around you. You're not the only one alone. Remember, the relationship wasn't working. If there hadn't been many unhappy moments with him, you wouldn't have left.

Recognize Your Positive Steps

Though the challenges of rebuilding a social life are significant, being single can have its perks. You get to decide where you eat dinner and when you clean the refrigerator. You get to be in charge of what you do with your life and how you spend your money. If you want to vacation in the Amazon, trekking into jungles that he'd hate, go for it. You're making progress if you can accept and grieve whatever social connections you've lost—mutual friends, his family, and so on. Congratulate yourself whenever you take the high road if you hear that someone is saying bad things about you or your behavior. It takes a strong person to ignore these comments, but you (and your children) will be better for it in the long run. Celebrate any positive steps you take to create a life without him, to meet new people, to make new friends—to move on.

- **You're not building a new life:** If you can't make yourself do things alone.
- **You're building a new life:** If you recognize the poor choices you made and you're ready to change.

Exercises and Affirmations

At this point, it's important to focus on finding new social connections. As a starting point, join a synagogue, a temple, or a church with which you share similar beliefs. If you're agnostic, find a study group, or start one, and explore your personal life philosophy. This is the moment to see beyond your personal struggle. It'll give you a bigger perspective and make your challenges seem less overwhelming in comparison. You may find that you can build new friendships with the people you meet in these settings.

chapter thirteen

Parenting After a Breakup

Things to Consider

- Are you still trying to direct the kind of parent he is?
- Does your form of believing in your kids involve your telling them what to do all the time, despite their heading toward, or already being in, adolescence?
- Is your parenting input the last way you can interact with your former mate?
- Letting go of how your children handle their father can be freeing.

Rebuilding a new life for yourself is a tall task . . . and helping your children understand how *their* lives will change adds a whole other dimension. They will need their questions answered, their fears calmed, and their doubts about your (or your partner's) love eliminated. You may need to approach each child differently, depending on his or her age and personality. What's most important is to consistently remind them that the breakup is not their fault and that both parents will continue to love them. In order to present a confident and united front, it's essential that you and your partner understand the realities of parenting after a breakup.

What You Can Control

The bad news, which we'll get to next, is that there are a lot of things you can't control regarding parenting after a breakup. The good news is that you can control how YOU parent. You can model good, mature behavior; listen to your kids and communicate with them at age-appropriate levels about what's going on; and do your best to create a normal life for them, post-breakup.

What You Can't Control

Perhaps the most difficult reality to accept is that you can't make your ex-partner parent the way you think he should. This may seem wrong, but it's true. You must accept his behavior and what the courts give you. He's as involved as he wants to be. He can be as good or as bad a parent as he wants to be. Looking back, have you ever had the power to change the way he parents or the way he does anything else? The sad reality is that now that the two of you are splitting up, you have even *less* power.

The Legal System

The legal system attempts to help establish and reinforce your children's safety and settle big parental arguments, but it can't do much more. Don't expect the courts to back you up on what you want him to do or to slap his hand when—in your judgment—he's not a good parent. The law wasn't designed for that (and it wouldn't be any good at it, anyway).

> ### The Courts Can't Work Magic
> The court system isn't magic and doesn't always make the decision you think it should. Know the limitations of the legal process. The court can't make your ex be the kind of parent you want him to be.

The court system will decide with whom kids live and how often you get visitation, but they don't always do this any better than the fighting parents would. The process will likely be time-consuming, expensive, and frustrating. Once you have a decision, you may not feel great about it, but unless you want to appeal (which may not even work), you must accept the terms and give it a shot.

Quiz: How Do You Feel about His Parenting?

On a scale of one to five (with one meaning you disagree strongly and five meaning you agree strongly), answer the following questions:

1. You're worried about his parenting. _____
2. You feel you should still have input into how he parents. _____
3. You think there needs to be more legal oversight of how your children's father treats them. _____
4. You think he should at least listen to your comments and observations about your children's daily life with him. _____
5. You want to be able to have veto power over the person your ex dates and, therefore, with whom your children spend time. _____

If you scored 20 or more points: Your ex-spouse's parenting is a big concern for you, and you probably don't have anything at all to say about it.

If you scored 11–19 points: It will take some adjusting for you to accept that you and your ex are no longer parenting together. Give yourself a break.

If you scored 5–10 points: You and your ex-spouse are usually on the same page in terms of parenting style.

His Parenting Choices

After you split up with your children's father, it can be difficult to accept that, while you both love your kids, you will no longer parent as a team. Even parents who work very hard not to let their relationship issues spill over onto their children have to work with the reality that individual parenting choices are now just that—individual. If the two of you decide to maintain an amicable interaction for the sake of your kids, you'll need to remind yourself that the only part of parenting over which you have any say is that which directly impacts your children's physical safety and well-being. If they're fed, clothed, and not being abused, you can't say anything about how your ex is parenting.

You can try guilting your ex into parenting the way you think he should, but this is a poor method—at best—of ensuring your children's well-being. Now that your ex isn't your mate anymore, he cares even less about what you think and may intentionally refuse to do what you want. You can't (if you ever could) make him act in the ways you think he ought to act. If he still wants an amicable relationship with you (or if he still has hope that you'll change your mind and get back together with him), he'll care more about what you think regarding the kids.

Were you the one who gave 85 percent of the care to the kids when the two of you were together? The bad news is that you still only get minimal input into how he parents now. You don't get to insist that your ex make the kids brush their teeth. You don't get to decide what friends the children hang out with when they're with him. You don't get any say in how they dress when they come from his house.

You have input in their medical and dental care. Depending on your particular divorce agreement, you may get to be part of the decision about which school they attend. That's usually about it.

Unfortunately, it's very difficult to talk with your ex about his parenting style. If you feel you must raise an issue, be sure to keep your parenting requests and suggestions separate from comments about his personal life. Mention your concerns about your kids, but don't tell him how to conduct his dating life, and drop both subjects altogether if you get a heated response.

His Future Romances

The biggest challenge of this new parenting reality may come when your ex starts dating. Now you have a second person you can't control but whose behavior and actions affect the well-being and happiness of your children. Please see page 207 for more on handling his new relationships.

Isabel's Story:

I was okay with whenever Zack wanted to see the kids. From the time of our divorce, I didn't make a big stink when he wanted to switch days or if he wanted to take them on a fishing trip with his mom. I went out of my way to make sure they still had access to their dad.

But when Cammie came in the picture, it got ridiculous. Zack started switching and skipping his visitation times constantly. He was going out of town with his new girlfriend or going to see her in one of her plays or something. Then, he started taking her with him when he would take the kids to see their grandparents. They'd come back and tell me that he and Cammie shared a room at Nana and Papa's!

The kids were clearly uncomfortable with this arrangement, but Zack just didn't care. Pretty soon, Cammie was with him all the time when he had the kids. It was like Zack didn't care if he saw his kids alone or not. Our children are in middle school. Kids start growing up early these days, but the last thing they need is their father's dates staying over. I'd never do that to them. It's just too confusing.

But when I talked with Zack about it, he wouldn't even listen. When we were in a relationship together, we agreed that kids needed values. They need to realize that having sex too early or jumping too quickly into a relationship can be dangerous. Now, it's like Zack wasn't even there when we made these decisions. He's got a girlfriend who he introduced right away to the kids and who he openly sleeps with. The kids notice all this! How can he expect them not to make bad sexual decisions when he's so blatant about screwing around?

It's just so frustrating to me that he doesn't even seem to care about how he's affecting the kids. If he has to change one little bit of his life to be a better parent, he's just not interested!

It can seem wrong and really upsetting, but when you split up from your children's father, you don't get to tell him how to parent or whom he can date. This is a reality you can't fight. Isabel's ex isn't required to make dating decisions in accordance with Isabel's values. She needs to keep quiet regarding her opinions of his new girlfriend.

She can, however, encourage her children to share their concerns with their father. Remember that kids sometimes tell a parent what they think the parent wants to hear. Isabel's children might not be as uncomfortable with his girlfriend sleeping over as they're telling Isabel. They may just know that Isabel isn't okay with it, and they are complaining to *align with her*. Kids do this. Don't give them grief about it, but don't go for the bait. Isabel needs to be as neutral as she can be when her children complain to her, neither defending their father nor attacking him. After they've vented, she can gently encourage her children to talk with their dad about their feelings. This empowers the kids, if they really are upset about Cammie.

Don't Refuse Him Access to the Kids

If you agreed with your ex about most things, the two of you wouldn't be splitting up. Since you are breaking up, you *really* don't agree, so don't expect that coparenting will go smoothly, either. Yes, this sounds depressing, but it's important to understand the reality that most women face post-breakup. Sure, some ex-partners get along well enough to calmly discuss these matters, but many don't. Keep in mind that *power struggles between you and him don't benefit anyone*. It only hurts the kids. Still, they can be very difficult to avoid.

Start Doing This

Repeat this mantra to yourself. Say it over and over, if need be: "I am not with him anymore. I can't tell him how to parent."

The most common power struggle is you two arguing about his access to the children. No matter how much you disagree with his parenting style, *don't limit his access to the kids*. You can only do this if he's actively hurting them (see page 205 for more on how to handle abusive situations). Unless his actions are actually harmful to the children (this includes abusing them as well as his driving drunk, or otherwise impaired, when the kids are in the car), your kids need their father in their life. Even if he's twisted and dysfunctional, they still need him in their lives, if only to later decide for themselves they want nothing to do with him.

ASK YOURSELF:
1. Is my children's father really a bad parent, or is he just a different kind of parent than I am?
2. Am I having a hard time with my kids meeting my ex's dates because *I'm* struggling with him dating?
3. Am I in denial about my children truly being abused by their father?
4. Can I separate my ex's parenting from our relationship issues?

Because raising children is something you've done together up till now, it can be very difficult to separate how you parent from how he parents. You need to work at viewing the two things apart from one another. You get to leave him, but he's always your children's father and, as such, he has inherent rights and inherent significance to your children.

> ### Hindsight Is 20/20
> Don't beat yourself up if the father of your children, the man you chose, isn't a good parent. You didn't know this when you made a baby. Give yourself a break.

Don't think you're doing your kids a favor by blocking their father's access to them. They won't appreciate your interference or the power struggles they'll witness; they'll instead be frustrated, resentful, and angry at you. The kids will believe he is wonderful, unless they find out differently for themselves. Most people want to believe their parents are good people.

Above all, it's important for kids to have their father in their lives. As a 2009 Florida International University study found, fathers are vital to raising happy, healthy, and successful children. Consider:

- Fathers have a different communication style than moms. This broadens kids' experience.
- Children with a dad who's active in their lives have higher self-esteem. Girls with involved fathers are more likely to avoid early pregnancy and to stay in school.
- Children with involved fathers get better grades in school.
- Having an involved father leads to lower levels of depression.
- Children with involved fathers exhibit fewer behavioral problems.

Fathers are important to children. All the research points to this. Unless your ex is harmful to them, your children need him in their lives. Don't get hung up on the SuperMom fallacy; you're not the only parent they need.

Making sure your children have a relationship with their father, however, isn't your job. You can make sure he can see them if he wants, but if he refuses, you can't make it happen. The appropriate action on your part depends on the kids' age. Younger children will need you to communicate for them (for example, tell their father when the kids will be available to see them); older kids will need to work this out for themselves. Just make sure you don't block access to their father. You're responsible for following the arrangements set by the courts, but you don't need to bend over backward to keep him involved if he has no interest. Be reasonable.

Keep Your Children Out of Abusive Situations

The one scenario under which you can deny the father of your children access is if you suspect or know he is abusing them. If you have evidence that he's sexually abusing the kids or beating them (to the point of leaving photographable marks), report him to authorities and eliminate his access to the children—but talk to your lawyer first. If you suspect abuse but aren't certain, immediately seek the help of a professional (your lawyer or a health professional) before taking further action.

Most women know this, but it's good to remember that you must report suspected abuse—it's against the law not to do so. Don't hesitate, even if your child is accusing someone close to you, whom you can't believe would do this. Report it.

This is very important, both for your relationship with your child and for your continued presence in your child's life. You must protect your child. If state child services get involved and you didn't report your child's outcry, you look like an unfit parent. As distressing and jarring as it is to find that a loved one has done unthinkable things to your child, you need to believe the child. Children rarely make up this kind of thing.

What Is Sexual Abuse of a Child?

Sexual abuse occurs when an older child (as little as two years old), a youth, or an adult uses a child or youth for his or her own sexual gratification. Incest, wherein a child is sexually violated by a parent, parental figure, older sibling, or other relative, is included in this definition. Sadly, sexual abuse is perpetrated most often by a family member or friend of the family. Stranger abuse, which parents most fear and which gets big media coverage, is a relatively rare occurrence.

Ignoring an outcry means that you're compromising your relationship with your child. Your child won't forget that you didn't trust him, even if you eventually do your best to keep the perpetrator away from the child.

On the other hand, don't go overboard looking for signs that your children have been sexually abused. Just because you have a very conflicted relationship with their father, and may even hate him, doesn't make him a child molester. Your kids won't benefit from your overreacting all the time, either. Don't think the worst of him . . . unless the child outright tells you that something bad has happened.

Don't Use the Kids

Working out your issues with your ex-partner through your kids will cause your relationship with the children to suffer.

Make sure you view your children as separate from your relationship with their father. Don't use the kids to maintain a connection, although this can feel very natural and be difficult to avoid if you still want the relationship (you just want it to be better). Unless your children are young and need your help, it's not your job to buy Father's Day gifts for your children to give your ex. If one of your children is an infant, he or she won't know about Father's Day and Christmas. Don't think you have to buy a gift for your ex unless your child can participate in the process.

> ### Separate Is Better
> Try hard to keep your feelings for their father separate from your interaction with your kids. They deserve the right to work this out themselves . . . and they won't thank you for getting in the middle of it.

Keep both your anger and your longing regarding your former relationship from polluting your children's interaction with their father. Go for neutral. When you're thrown together with your ex at a school event or a baseball game, smile at him in a random way and sit on the other side. If he greets you, respond and keep it brief. Don't go to either extreme, either cuddling up next to him or rigidly refusing to acknowledge his presence. Your emotion is your business, and you have all the capacity you need to sort through it without involving the children.

Handling Your Kids' Stepmother and/or the Women He Dates

It can seem strange for someone else to date your ex and have sex with him. (Unless, of course, he was tramping around when you were married. Then, it's not strange.) If you're truly over the relationship, it shouldn't matter to you whom he dates and you certainly shouldn't need to talk badly about him or the woman (women!) he dates. If you find yourself having a negative reaction to his new romance, ask yourself why. Do you have actual reasons to believe that she's evil? If not, consider that the problem might be on your end.

His relationships can present other challenges if he remarries. What if your kids want to call their stepmother "Mom"? Don't freak out. Let the kids make the decision. You may be convinced that your evil ex asked the kids to call her that when they already have you. Still, suck it up and don't give your kids trouble for calling her "Mom." Don't act hurt or weepy, even if you feel that way. Most mothers don't want their children calling anyone else "Mom," but think about the situation from your kids' standpoint.

You want your kids to have a good relationship with whomever he's dating. *You* might harbor resentment if this relationship started while he was still with you, but regardless, you want your kids to have a good relationship with her. Again, since you should keep your feelings about him separate from your kids' relationship with him, you need to deal with that resentment (and any lingering feelings about your breakup) on your own.

If your kids and their stepmother get off on the right foot, their life will be smoother and happier. Stepmothers who have it in for a kid—a situation that can happen if stepmoms take out their resentment for the birth mother on the kids—can make life hell. (Remember Cinderella?)

Keep things in perspective. You're their mom and you always will be. This isn't a competition. Remember these facts:

- No one can take your place.
- You're their mom. (Biological or adopted, it doesn't matter.)

- You've loved them since they were tiny. You have seniority.
- Even if they seem to like her better, don't freak out. They're dealing with the separation, too. It's natural that they'd want their father's significant other to like them.
- Kids need to separate from their parents (mom, too). They need to know they can make it on their own.

Since your ex's relationship is his own business, keep your nose out of it. And don't even think of involving the kids—never force them to ask the new girlfriend personal questions so you can find out more about her.

 Say This to Yourself
"I don't need to allow my feelings for him or my feelings about whoever he's dating to determine whether or not I make it hard for him to see our children."

One of the most important parenting jobs is to empower children. They need to see their strengths, such as doing well in school, and to have self-confidence, so they can say "no" to drugs. You want your kids to feel strong enough to handle life. You've probably told them they're beautiful and wonderful and terrific. Now, act like it. Act like your children can make choices on their own. You may not agree with all these decisions (let's face it, you *won't* agree with all of them), but it is hugely important that your actions reflect your belief in their capacity to make good choices. How they handle separated parents, and parents who are dating other people, is their call.

Believe in them, even if they're screwing up. (You have. You *do*.) Give your kids the ultimate gift—your unconditional love and support. Let them make their own decisions. Even about *her*.

What to Do If Your Children Want to Live with Dad

More and more, fathers are occupying the role of significant caretaker. Some don't, though, and it can be jarring for children to decide to live with a parent who's had very little to do with their upbringing.

Whether your children are responding to a closeness they feel with their involved, loving dad (maybe they don't want him to think they love you more!) or they're trying to get close to a dad they've never known, they have their reasons—and those reasons might not have anything to do with you. In rare cases, your children might choose to live with their father if you've had a very conflicted relationship with them. This isn't typically the case, however.

Support Their Decision

Some school-age children simply have curiosity about living with their noncustodial parent. They wonder what it will be like, how they'll feel, and how it'll be different from living with you. The court system begins allowing children to have input regarding the custodial parent when the children get older; generally, when their age hits double digits. You, too, should begin taking their choices into account. Listen to what they have to say—especially when their decision is more than a whim and isn't just blurted out when one or more of them are mad at you and want to get your attention.

As much as you might feel rejected, their request typically isn't about you or your parenting. Children just need to know both parents. Be strong; let them go. This is a hard thing for many mothers to face, but it also can be the most loving act you're called to do. Remember that an involved father is optimal for your children's best mental health. This means he loves them, too, and wants to see them every day, just as you do. They love you, but they love him, too. They might simply want to live with him. It doesn't mean they don't still love you.

Don't Make the Children Choose

Don't make your kids choose between loving their father and loving you. Even if you're worried about your children now and are sure that they need your assistance, it's important to realize that you're working your way out of the parent job. That's how it should be. You want your children to grow into a strong, independent adults.

Mariah's Story:

Justin and I were married for almost sixteen long years. I really tried hard to make it work, but when we finally decided to separate, I was relieved to be out of the constant fighting.

It was hard, at first, to adjust to life on my own and to keep a stable world for my two kids. When my daughter graduated high school and went away to college in a neighboring state, I knew she'd be homesick for a while. But I have no doubt that Ashley's ready to start this next part of her life.

After Ashley headed off to college, Aiden, my fifteen-year-old son, suddenly said that he wanted to live with his father. I was totally blown away. Aiden had never even said anything about living with his dad. But now he said he only had a few years of school left before he goes to college himself and he wants to live with his dad before he goes out on his own.

I didn't even know he was thinking about this. It's really upset me.

I called to accuse Justin of trying to steal my son away. I mean, I'd thought this would be mine and Aiden's time to bond while it's just the two of us. But Justin said that Aiden brought the idea up to him. He's recently remarried, and his new wife has two sons of her own. Justin said Aiden's request was unexpected, but welcomed.

I wonder if Aiden's worried that his dad will now get closer and spend more time with the new stepsons.

But I couldn't stand in his way and fight him moving to his dad's. I knew he'd never forgive me if I did that. So, he moved in with Justin and, all of a sudden, I was faced with an empty nest. I spent sleepless nights worrying that I wouldn't be able to steer my son through the sometimes difficult teenage choices. His dad worked long hours when we were married. What if he does that now? I wasn't sure he would have the time to give our son, and it's important to have an involved, concerned parent at this point in a kid's life.

There were days when I thought I should just tell Aiden that he couldn't live with his father and he should move back home. Of course, in my saner moments I knew that, at his age, Aiden could legally choose to live with his father. The law gave him that right, but I hated the thought of him not living out his teenage years with me.

When I thought about this more calmly, I realized this wasn't just about where Aiden was better off . . . I was nervous about being on my own! For years, I've talked about the things I'll do when the children are grown up and don't need me to take care of them. I've been excited about not having to be responsible all the time. I guess I just hadn't planned on it happening so quickly.

Even if she has concerns about him living with his father full-time, Mariah will do her relationship with Aiden more harm if she tries to keep him from living with his father. She needs to face this transition gracefully, even if she doesn't feel prepared.

It is important that she encourage her son in trying out his wings. After all, she wants him to be a successful adult, even if he has left the nest earlier than she'd planned. Although she's very aware of what she's missing with her son living elsewhere, she can tremendously strengthen her relationship with her son simply by believing in him. If by some chance he wants to return to live with her, she can welcome him without criticizing his desire to live with his dad or obviously rejoicing in his dad's failure to be all Aiden wanted.

She needs to visit and see Aiden regularly. Take him and his buddies to dinner. Go to his ball games or debates. She can show her support in many ways, and that's what parenting at this time of a child's life is all about. He may not return to live with her, but he'll always know she believes in him.

This Is Your Chance to Redefine Yourself

Sometimes children decide to live with their father at an even younger age than Aiden. If your children move in with your ex, you don't have to see this as a disaster. If the children are living with him, he gets his turn on the front lines of parenting. That means you get the chance—either when they move in with him or go off to college—to be a great noncustodial parent. This is an important role. Not having children to care for daily will also allow you to live a different life.

For the first time in a long time, you get to put some energy into being More-Than-Mom. You get to develop new friendships, new hobbies, and new talents. You get to redefine yourself. You knew this shift was coming, but it can occur sooner than you'd planned. Take advantage of the moment to broaden and develop your life.

Recognize Your Positive Steps

You're committed to being the best parent you can be, even when the situation is complicated by breaking up with your child's father. You're making progress if you can let go of trying to control your ex, and accept that you can't tell him how to parent or whom to date. You're also acting in a mature and responsible manner if you can separate your feelings for your husband from your children's lives and keep them out of disagreements and lingering resentments. Keeping an open mind about your ex's new girlfriend shows that you're accepting the breakup and want your kids to have a good relationship with her. If your children decide to live with their father, demonstrate to them that you believe in them by supporting their choice. This is the greatest gift a parent can give a child.

These changes aren't easy to swallow, but with every small step, you're moving ahead with a new life—and that's something to be proud of.

- **You're not letting go if:** You're still caught up in trying to influence how your ex parents. This can indicate that you're not *done* with your former relationship or, at the very least, that you have little faith in your children working this out.

- **You're moving ahead as a divorced parent if:** You've finished grieving the end of your relationship with your ex and can allow him to parent however he chooses.

Exercises and Affirmations

Ask your three best friends what they'd say is your best quality, and listen to their feedback without dismissing what they say. Really consider their answers, particularly if they repeat what you've heard from others is a strength in you. Then be conscious of this. *Own it.* And as you begin looking around for other guys that interest you, be aware that you have good things to offer.

Then, go shopping to get something that makes you feel pretty. If you're on a limited budget (which many newly separated singles are), look for a low-cost boost, such as a new nail polish color or a lipstick shade. If your finances will stand it, buy a flattering new outfit. This is practice for putting yourself first and taking care of yourself. Taking care of yourself helps keep you happy and healthy, which enables you to be a better parent.

chapter fourteen

Post-Breakup Survival Strategies

Things to Consider

- Are you conflicted about what's happening with your ex?
- Do you really want to move forward?
- Is the future really scary? Defining yourself separately from him can be more jolting than fighting with him, but it's a challenge you can conquer.

Having left a previous relationship can feel like you've let go of an anchor—you may feel free for the first time in a long time. You might also feel adrift and be scared by all your choices and emotional baggage. Leaving a committed relationship might have been the right choice for you, but it's natural to grieve aspects of yourself that were also left. Some of these you'll gladly throw to the winds; some parts you may miss terribly. Learning some general coping strategies will help you face these times with more confidence, support, and positive energy.

Quiz: Are You Trying to Move On?

On a scale of one to five (with one meaning you disagree strongly and five meaning you agree strongly), answer the following questions:

1. As a holiday approaches, you've started thinking about good holiday moments between the two of you and you're missing him. _____
2. You've made some poor choices since the two of you split up and you're wondering if you really are better off without him. _____
3. Even though you know you've tried to fix the relationship before and it hasn't gotten better, you're wondering now if you should go back and try again. _____
4. You're not sure how to move forward in your life. _____
5. You wonder if life with him was as good as you can expect from future relationships. _____

If you scored 20 or more points: You're struggling with fear, and possibly depression, but that doesn't mean you can't find a healthier place.

If you scored 11–19 points: You're trying to believe in yourself, but you are having a hard time remembering that you have options, and you don't know how to feel better.

If you scored 5–10 points: You struggled to make the decision, but you see that leaving the relationship was best for you.

Choose Your Coping Mechanisms

When you're deeply sad, unhealthy behaviors can seem to bring comfort. Don't cave in to this temptation—it'll only make matters worse. Drinking, smoking pot, and using food as a crutch can lead to more problems than you originally faced coming out of the relationship. While under the influence, you can make some really bad decisions.

Here are a few healthy coping behaviors to try:

- Exercise, but not to excess.
- Help others in need; it heals your soul, too.
- Be moderate in your behaviors.
- Remember, the pain will get less and less as you go on with your life.

Choose your coping behaviors carefully. Seek comfort, but don't seek things that will bring you huge, new headaches. You don't want to wake up married to a stranger.

Beware of Your Old Patterns

Be mindful if you notice yourself falling into old bad habits—such as sleeping with an old boyfriend or maxing out your credit cards. Old patterns are powerful, but if they were good for you, you wouldn't need to change them now. It can also seem natural to seek out others who *don't* actually help you—family members who have destructive effects on you, or friends who bring out the worst in you.

At the bottom of this tendency to seek unhealthy outlets is a sneaky belief that maybe you're not worth much, anyway. *What does it matter if I sleep with that stranger or go into debt? I'm a failure anyway.* Dismiss this thought. *It isn't true*, and you'll only make decisions you will regret. You are a worthwhile person and you deserve a happy life. You can create a better life for yourself.

Don't Make Major Changes Just Yet

You might want to move across the country, adopt a child, or quit your job immediately after the two of you say a final good-bye. These might be good, functional things to do, but hold off on those decisions for a few months. Think carefully about your motivations before you make big changes. This is a good time for some actions, but you need to take an objective look at why you're inclined to do them.

You're now in the middle of a whirlwind called "relationship loss." Even if you and he had big conflicts over some specific choices, and you want to jump into those choices now that you and he are no longer together, take a deep breath first. Give yourself a moment.

This is an adjustment period. *Allow some time for him to leave your heart and your head before you commit to someone or something else. Let yourself heal.*

Take Care of Yourself

Although the urge is to find comfort when you're stressed with new life challenges, some people gravitate toward comfort behaviors that don't help overall. This is the time that you need to do what is best for you. Some people have the urge to cry all the time; others isolate themselves like an injured animal. Try to act in moderation, but let yourself engage in behaviors that work for you and are healthy. Even if others tell you that you don't need to cry or that you should make sure you're always in a crowd, you still need to let yourself cry—if you feel like it—or spend some time just with your thoughts. Work to incorporate your style of comforting yourself with other behaviors that might also be good for you.

During your adjustment to the breakup, treat yourself like you're convalescing after a long illness. Go for long, slow walks. Drink herbal tea (if you're so inclined). Sleep. There is no magic time frame for dealing with a loss. It is a very individual thing. But you need to deal with the transition—feel the loss, feel your own strength, realize you can do this—before you scurry into the next phase.

Spiritual Self-Care

In times of transition, it's a good idea to rely on your spiritual beliefs as a moral compass. Religion can be a strong support. Check to see what your religious affiliation offers in the way of spiritual development, and get involved.

Some people find organized religions to be unsatisfying and prefer to step outside that experience. Spiritual beliefs aren't confined to an external structure. You might find more satisfaction in Native American spiritual practices or in Wiccan beliefs. For some individuals, seeking a spiritual group is natural. Others choose to spend time in spiritual reflection by themselves. Whatever your belief or your preference of activity, this is a good time to reconnect.

Start Doing This

Explore your own spiritual beliefs. If you attend the church of your childhood, make sure you look at it from your adult perspective. You don't have to agree with your parents or your ex. You're fully capable of deciding what is fulfilling to you.

Church groups frequently offer an outlet for those who wish to study and explore their faith. Participating in these sessions can be very helpful when you're making changes in your life.

Physical Self-Care

The stress of ending a relationship can have different effects on different people. Some individuals eat more to comfort themselves in difficult times. Some can't eat at all. Giving attention to your physical concerns is very important.

You may not want to get off the couch, but you'll feel better in the long run if you get active. You might want to start a workout program at a new gym or join neighbors in walking every day. Figure out what works best for you, and get moving. The benefits of physical activity are many. In addition to helping your heart and your weight, regular exercise has been shown to raise the body's own endorphins. James Blumenthal, PhD, found in a 1999 Duke University study that engaging in consistent aerobic activity can have the same effect as taking an antidepressant.

Elizabeth's Story:

Grant and I were together for sixteen years. The last ten were pretty rocky, though. We argued over money and how to spend our free time. We argued about each other's families. We even fought about what church to go to. We both wanted to go to church, but we didn't like the same one. When our sixteen-year-old daughter, Erynn, asked me why her dad and I were still together, I had to ask myself the same question. I guess I just hate giving up, but I finally had to accept that this wasn't ever going to change. We weren't going to get beyond it.

The day Grant moved out was really hard, but I realized later that I was glad I didn't come home to an argument every evening. That was a relief.

Still, this relationship was the only thing I'd known for a long time. I didn't even know how to be single anymore. Some of my friends wanted to introduce me to men right away and get me to jump immediately back in the dating pool. I wasn't eager, though. I felt I'd mourned the relationship with Grant and I certainly don't regret ending it, but I wasn't sure I was ready to start another relationship. My friends seemed like they were always with one guy or another or looking for a guy. It seemed exhausting. I just didn't have the energy.

Then, I realized I was laying around every night. I came home from work, ate something out of the freezer, and crashed in front of the tube. I decided to take a friend's advice and join a Pilates class. It was jolting at first. I didn't realize how out of shape I'd gotten, but soon I wasn't suffering so much after a class. Little by little, I started getting physically stronger and I was certainly more flexible. I'm liking how I look more, too. I joined a gym near my work and started to lift weights several times a week. It's not all that fun, but I've started feeling better. Sometime in the near future, I might be up for finding some more people to hang out with. I feel like I'm waking up after a long, long nap.

Elizabeth has been worn down by the unsuccessful effort she expended on the relationship with Grant. By putting some time and energy into herself, she's being a good role model for her daughter and taking the first steps toward creating a new life. She needs to look at her own emotions and see if the hesitance she feels about dating has anything to do with her feeling like a failure for not being able to fix the relationship. There is no forward movement in life without taking chances, and that involves the risk of not succeeding. Elizabeth has to accept that relationships are complex and involve two people. Now that she's worked on herself for a while, she needs to think about venturing into dating. It's important that she learns to believe in herself.

Emotional Self-Care

There are few things as lonely as being newly single after a breakup. In the midst of your conflict, you may have disconnected from friends and family, but you need both now. It is vital that you have a social network. It's easy to get misdirected—and in an effort to make the relationship a priority, you might have invested less in the support systems. You need to spend time with people who enjoy you. This strengthens you for whatever challenges you face.

Use Your Support Systems

In our splintered society, you might struggle to find connections with others. You aren't alone in this difficulty. Some individuals do have close friendships, girlfriends who hang out in groups, or pseudo-family connections (your mother was married to his uncle, your sister dated his best friend, and so on). This may not be the case for you, though. Either way, friends are an important part of your support system.

Reviving Old Connections

You may have—through dealing with the challenges of the relationship—disconnected from the people or groups that had previously been your foundation. Did you stop spending time with family members whom your ex didn't like or who pointed out the limitations of your relationship with your ex? Some people in difficult relationships stop going to church and give up hobbies or interests that brought them into contact with others.

It's possible that your ex felt jealous or threatened by these other people in your life and, with the sorry state of your relationship with him, it would make sense if you felt (just a teensy bit) flattered by this. Then, when you and he were getting along, you could have disconnected from other people, since it felt like he was all you needed.

 Say This to Yourself
"I can be a good friend, even if I've forgotten that people like hanging out with me."

You need these connections now. Actually, you always needed these connections, but this is a time to re-establish them if you've let them lapse. Don't let your guilt or embarrassment over dropping friends and activities keep you from knocking on those doors again. Remember, you're not the only one who's struggled with relationships. Most friends and family will understand. There were probably some hurt feelings, but many fences can be mended, particularly if you say briefly that you're learning from your mistakes.

At least attempt to reconnect. Go back to your old dance class, rejoin the charity group you once belonged to, or visit the business networking group you used to hang with. Give these friendships a chance to revive. Don't let your having withdrawn from them keep you from reconnecting.

Making New Connections

Many newly single people don't have solid support systems. There are a variety of reasons for this situation:

- You've moved away from your friends.
- Your family is really dysfunctional.
- Your relationship troubles made you too distracted to nurture friendships, so they fell by the wayside.

Regardless of how you ended up in this situation, it's time to build a new network of friends. This is an important step in forging a complete, independent life for yourself.

Keep at It
New connections can be difficult to forge, but don't give up. Seek out an activity or two that interest you, and invest some time in them. *Remember*, you're not looking for a date. You're looking for friends and people you can enjoy spending time with.

Pursue New Interests

One way to build new friendships is to join a group with an activity you enjoy as its central focus. This interest connects you to other people who like the same thing. Here are some ideas to get you started:

- Join a religious or spiritual group.
- Join a gym.
- Take up kick-boxing or another sport you enjoy.
- Take a ceramics class.
- Become a Big Sister.
- Volunteer.
- Go back to school.

These are the beginnings of creating a support system. It isn't automatic, however. You walk into these situations as a stranger, and you have to give emotional connection some time to develop. Be consistent in attending these activities and be sure that you'll really enjoy the focus of the group. Don't choose a church just because it's on your way home from work, especially if you totally disagree with its ideology.

It's important that you open yourself to connecting with others. This means looking for shared interests and listening to others when they talk about their interests. Pouring out your life story or telling people the gory details of your failed relationship won't create instant friends. Give it some time. Connections don't happen automatically or easily, but they will come with time and nurturing.

What a Breakup Can Teach You

It never feels good to fail. You wanted this relationship to work and it didn't. This can feel like the most personal kind of failure, but put it in perspective—relationships are difficult. Many good, intelligent people have failed relationships. Still, you don't want to repeat this experience, if you can help it. So, take your failure by the scruff of the neck and shake it a little. Your former partner and you both contributed to this relationship. You can't fix his part, but you can work on yours.

> **Love Yourself**
> - Listen to your own assessment of yourself.
> - Realize that you need input from safe people.
> - It can't be all your fault.

It's very important that you approach your breakup without a lot of self-recrimination. Remorse and self-blame are counterproductive in the process and can actually keep you from seeing what you need to see. Avoidance of reality, in this kind of situation, is normal! Don't avoid learning, though. You need to learn what there is to learn from the experience to increase your chances of not repeating it.

Get a whole picture of what you contributed to the relationship— the good and the bad. There was some good, even if that's hard to find. You need to be able to see yourself with some accuracy. Your mother, your best friend, and your drinking buddies are all going to tell you that he's a jerk and you're better off without him. They may have started telling you this early in the conflict. This doesn't mean that *you're* perfect, either. Nevertheless, you're still a decent person. You deserve to see the issues that are holding you back.

- Ask your best friend to be honest with you and tell you what you could learn from your breakup. She won't be brutally honest, but she'll give you one perspective.
- Ask the most objective person you know what you can change about yourself. This may be awkward and difficult, but you will hear things that you need to know. (Remember—even the most objective friend or relative won't be totally objective, but she or he can tell you things you need to hear.)

- Join a self-help group at your church or community center. Then, talk about your recent experience in your relationship. Stress that you need to learn about yourself.
- Consider speaking to your minister, spiritual adviser, or a therapist. Ask what you can change to be a better partner next time.
- Don't take everything everyone says as absolute truth. It's true *from their perspective.*

Consider Professional Help

Sometimes, individuals feel overwhelmed after a relationship breakup. They have a hard time functioning from day to day or continue to have obsessive thoughts about their former mate. They have a hard time understanding what happened or how they contributed. If you find yourself in this situation, consider professional help. A good therapist can help you identify these behaviors and give you guidance on how to change them, if you're not certain.

Recognize Your Positive Steps

This is a tough, scary time for you, but just being here means you're brave—you've made the tough decision to leave your partner. You're making progress if you notice yourself resisting old patterns that didn't work for you in the past. It's okay to ask for support at this time—at first from longtime friends and family members, then from new friendships you build. Progress is also *avoiding* bad decisions. Sometimes maintaining the status quo is the right thing to do while you figure out your future.

You know that you are lovable, and that by learning what went wrong in your previous relationship, you're avoiding a repeat of it.

- **You're not coping well if:** You're rehashing everything that happened in your relationship.

- **You're coping well if:** You're focusing on how you can create a new life for yourself.

Exercises and Affirmations

Make a commitment to exercise. Join a gym, start a home workout routine, or take walks at least every other morning. This isn't about your weight or how you look; it's a stress reducer. Go for moderate rather than intense activity, and work on being consistent. Don't beat yourself up if you skip a day or a week. Just get back on track. Physical activity makes you more resilient and less prone to anxious, depressed thoughts.

chapter fifteen

Building Your New Life

Things to Consider

- Do you know you're stronger than you sometimes feel?
- Do you recognize that moving forward is almost always scary?
- Have you accepted that you deserve a healthy relationship? Healthy doesn't necessarily mean *easy* all the time . . . but there should be more happiness than anger!

Your life post-breakup can be both exciting and scary. After leaving him, being alone can feel naked and lonely at times. Some people jump into singlehood without missing a beat; others stand on the brink and wonder what the heck to do. What's most important is to focus on creating the life *you* want. Consider your needs first and make decisions that lead to your independence, happiness, and personal fulfillment.

Quiz: How Are You Approaching Change?

On a scale of one to five (with one meaning you disagree strongly and five meaning you agree strongly), answer the following questions:

1. You've been so caught up in your troubled relationship, you're not sure what you really want anymore. _____
2. You privately think you're a loser because you couldn't make the relationship work. _____
3. This isn't the time to expand. You're overloaded and overwhelmed. _____
4. You don't try new things. There's just too much risk. _____
5. You're not sure you should do the things you want to do, but your mate didn't like. Maybe he was right. _____

If you scored 20 or more points: You're afraid to go forward.

If you scored 11–19 points: Sometimes the new life ahead of you is exciting, and sometimes it's scary. You struggle to know the next best step.

If you scored 5–10 points: You are ready to build your new life.

Set New Goals

As you start your new life post-breakup, it's time to sit down and focus on what you want to accomplish or feel in the upcoming months and years. You get to make your life the way *you* want it to be now, so be proactive. (If you're not a goal-setter, at least take some time to think about how you can craft this new life of yours.) To start, look back at where you've been. Doing so can be educational and can help you see what you need to do next.

Then, consider the following aspects of your life:

Career

If you love the job you're in now, great; stay there. If, on the other hand, you've thought for a while now that advancement could be interesting, this is the time to take the plunge. A challenge can help spur you forward. This is the moment to have faith in your abilities . . . even if you don't necessarily *feel* all that great about yourself. (Remember, emotions aren't always the complete reality.) Examine the possibilities. What does forward movement look like for *you*? This is a very individual choice. Sometimes, it means a promotion in a field where you already work; sometimes, you want to switch professions altogether. Don't do this on the spur of the moment, but do consider change.

You might need to go back to school to get a degree to make you more attractive to prospective employers. This return to academia might be scary, but that in itself isn't a reason not to go back to school. You have more capacity than you give yourself credit for.

Move to a New Town

If you've always wanted to live in a different place than where you lived with your ex, this is the moment. Whether you want to move someplace new or move back to your hometown, you can begin making the decisions for yourself now. It can be scary, but have faith in your survival skills. You can do it.

Victoria's Story:

When Cal and I got out of school, he got a job in Nevada, so we moved there. But I never liked the desert. I'd grown up in Ohio and I longed for trees! I've hated the landscape the whole time we've been here, but that wasn't the worst. Cal and I got along okay the first six months, but after that, it got rough. We stuck it out for almost two years, but then we had to make some decisions. Cal and I had tried to make things work, but it started to seem that he didn't like anything about me and, after a while, I didn't like him much.

So here I was having moved to this town for him and I wasn't with him anymore. I felt lonely, even though I knew it was better this way. My folks had left Ohio and retired to Florida. I didn't really want to live in Florida, so I stayed where I was out of uncertainty. After a while, I felt like I needed to find a new direction in my life. I started thinking about how I enjoyed the East coast, even the winters. Still, I'd put down roots here. I had a job that was okay, and some friends. I was still in Nevada even after Cal and I broke up, and I wasn't even sure why. Taking the chance to actually move to a place where I didn't know anyone, but really loved, took a big leap of faith.

Victoria acted on her belief in herself. In starting over in a new place with a new job and a new home, she's trusting in her own abilities. If it feels weird for a while, that's normal. *New* is unknown. This uncertainty can stimulate her to reach inside herself and find new depths. It can push her into taking steps she might otherwise hesitate to take. She can reach out to new neighbors and find new communities, start new hobbies, connect with new friends.

Commit to a New Pet

If you and your ex shared a pet that he now cares for, or he didn't like pets but you always wanted one, now is the time to find a new pet to love. Dog, cat, fish, whatever you want. Besides being fun, pets:

- Can help lower blood pressure, lower cholesterol levels, and reduce the risk of heart disease
- Can alleviate stress symptoms such as headaches, indigestion, and difficulty sleeping (research published in 2005 by the *British Medical Journal* indicates there is a connection between pet ownership and health benefits)
- Can help you get more physical exercise (if you have a dog or an energetic cat)
- Help safeguard against depression or loneliness
- Help improve social skills
- Help to ease loss

Think carefully before entering into this new relationship of pet to pet owner. You're making what may be a long-term commitment, and you don't want to do this on a whim. On the plus side, your pet will love you uncritically, and this relationship won't involve the challenges you've faced with your ex. On the negative side, owning a pet can tie you down and give you someone else to worry about when you need to be thinking about your own best interests.

Create New Holiday Traditions

Starting a new phase of your life necessarily means letting go of the old one . . . even the parts you liked. If you've left the relationship because *he* wanted to move on, you're probably experiencing rejection as well as relief. If *you're* the one who decided to leave, you may feel guilty. That's an ugly word—guilt—and you may feel you're being followed by a dark cloud you can't lift. Holidays bring guilt, regret, and a host of other emotions. Nonetheless, think carefully before you do something you'll later wish you hadn't done.

Significant days can leave you prey to sadness and despair. These times can actually bring fresh waves of sadness and loss. While you may have had your ugliest fights during the holidays (most people try too hard to be *Happy!* at the holidays), you might also have had "vacation amnesia." That happens when you go away for a vacation or when you enjoy the pretty moments of holidays, and see only the good things in the relationship. The realities of day-to-day living get blurry for some individuals during these happy times. Even when it hasn't worked out this way—such as when holidays or vacations were difficult times—you can fantasize about it. You might think, when under the influence of Christmas cookies or Halloween candy, that this time it will be different. This time, the two of you will recapture whatever originally brought you together.

Sorry, it doesn't work that way.

Problems don't go away just because you dress up and party together. Expensive gifts and stockings on the mantel don't make the issues disappear.

Start Doing This

Take a moment when you're alone and think about the worst holiday time you spent with him. If holidays were the only times that the two of you put aside your difficulties, think good and hard about bad times you had during the rest of the year. Then, remind yourself that you're making a better life now.

It can be sad to mark your relationship loss through annual events (your first Christmas apart; your first birthday alone), but that doesn't mean you were wrong to have ended the relationship. You may be at a New Year's Eve party and remember a New Year's Eve party the two of you attended in happier times. The memory can be painful, but it doesn't change anything.

Don't Invite Him

Excluding him can seem harsh, but it's usually not the best move to invite your ex to spend the holidays with you and the family—at least not immediately after breaking up. It can be confusing and sad. Celebrating together was the *old* reality. It's not how life is now, though. You need to move on to create a new "normal," and that means he's not part of your celebrations anymore.

If you have children together, it might seem as if having your ex over for Christmas morning, Hanukkah, or other holidays is the best choice *for your children*. You don't want the kids upset, and the kids want the family together again. *It's just one day* (night, weekend, whatever), you tell yourself. That's true, but it doesn't mean it's the right decision. Your children, as well as you and your ex, need to deal with this new reality. This is another "rip off the Band-Aid" moment: it's painful, but it's better to get the pain over with quickly (don't invite him!) than to drag it out (by trying to pretend you're together).

Think about What You Want

You both may have been good at putting on a happy face for the holidays and going through the motions while you were together, but that doesn't mean that faking it is a good idea now that you're officially separated. Think about these two facts:

- Holidays tend to be emotional times—both happy and sad. Don't forget that the feelings you feel at these times are not a complete picture. It's just one day.
- This is a time to make yourself happy. Do what's best for *you*. If you have kids, know that what's best for you is likely best for your children, too.

Remember that you're moving forward, not commemorating the past. If you have residual hope for fixing the relationship, it may pop up now. Look at it this way: if there's something left of the relationship, separate holidays will help you see what life will be without one another. You might not like that picture, and that may spur you to take the action you need to take, but don't make this decision until after the holidays. It's not a choice to make when you're still dealing with the emotional impact of the celebrations at this time of the year.

The Pointlessness of Drowning in Regret

During the holidays, you may tell yourself that your ex has no (decent) family beyond yours. You also may be thinking that it isn't fair that he's separated from the children at this special time. Maybe he didn't want the divorce; you initiated it. How could you take the holiday from him, too?

> ### *Holidays Are Complicated*
> Holidays can be exciting and fun, but remember that Norman Rockwell just painted pretty pictures. Life is way more complicated.

Regret goes both ways. If you think about the relationship, you'll probably realize you're not the only one with regrets. At holiday times, you can tend to look back and think *it wasn't so bad*. Yet if anyone were to seriously suggest you go back to him, you'd probably start remembering the problems. Instead of focusing on regrets or feeling bad about his current situation, remind yourself of how strong you were to make a good decision for yourself, and how you need to continue being strong to help both of you move on.

Plan Ahead
You can get a jump on holiday dilemmas by thinking now about the choices you'll face when those days and seasons come around. Think months ahead, not just weeks. That will make it easier to use your *smart brain*, the one that doesn't drown in regret over all the ways you could have been a better wife (and mother, if that applies). Birthdays, anniversaries, and holidays are times of high emotion. *They are not the time to be making big decisions.* Avoid emotional dilemmas by making some decisions well ahead of time.

ASK YOURSELF:
1. What will I miss most about him during the holiday celebration?
2. Will anything have changed, and will I miss him *after* the holiday?

3. Do I feel responsible for making him sad over the holiday?
4. Do I feel I owe it to my kids—or other family members—to include him in the holiday celebration?

If you look ahead and decide some of the do's and don'ts early, you'll have less stress later on.

 Say This to Yourself
"I hoped for happier times in this relationship and am sad that this is not the reality. But I need to think carefully before I get back with him. I need to remember that I don't have to stay sad."

Replacement Memories

To help combat any sadness and regret you feel, think carefully about how you can create new special times. This isn't a denial mechanism; it's part of moving on. You can create a new happiness, even when there's sadness behind you. Try these ideas:

- Go on vacations you always wanted to take, maybe to places that didn't interest him.
- Seek out new activities. Broaden your way of looking at celebrations.
- Consider spending time with different people than you may have before.

Don't Jump into a New Relationship

Yes, it's tempting to try to rebound quickly. You've been in a relationship (maybe one after another) and you're accustomed to being *with* someone, rather than being alone. Be careful, though. You may feel lonely, but the answer isn't to climb into bed with a whole new set of problems.

But They're New and Exciting!

It may seem like a good idea to try to deal with grief by swallowing it up with the excitement of another relationship. Coming bruised out of one relationship, you may doubt that anyone will want you. A new romantic interest can seem reassuring.

In the beginning, dating someone feels exciting. You can be gripped with the giddiness that comes with someone liking you. The new-relationship feeling is quite powerful. In its grip, you can be pulled into repeating your mistakes, but magnified ten times over. Remember, you don't know this person. You may have known him in some other non-relationship capacity (he was a friend from high school, you've known him at church, your children belong to the same Little League team), but you don't *know* him.

He may have issues that are bigger than the ones you dealt with in your former relationship. Since you don't know him, you don't know his devils. Leave the serious dating until you're clear of the previous guy.

Contemplating New Relationships?

If you've been in the process of ending your past relationship for a while, you might be ready to move on. Unfortunately, there is no magic timeline for when it's okay to date seriously again. But if you're not thinking about him all the time or looking for opportunities to talk to him or about him, you're probably getting closer to thinking about wanting a new relationship.

If you do decide to date again, date smart. Don't repeat the same mistakes that got you into the last situation. Don't date a man with the same issues as the one you're leaving.

You may find that as you come out of a committed relationship, you need some time and space to clear your head. You may not feel ready to jump back on the horse that just threw you. It's your call. You get to decide when you're ready to open yourself up to another relationship.

This is your life, and you are very capable of directing it.

ASK YOURSELF:

1. Am I afraid to start dating because I don't want to fail again?
2. Does behaving differently—in this relationship or a new one—scare me?
3. Do I really want to be a different person, or do I just want my significant other to be different?
4. Do I know where to start?

You may not have all the answers to these questions right away, but that's normal. Dating can be scary, and you might meet a few guys who aren't right for you. But you can learn a heck of a lot more from these "mistakes" than from never taking risks. If your first few dates post-breakup are less than exciting, don't get discouraged. Finding a new life partner is no less complicated and challenging than getting the right new job. Make sure you have reasonable expectations, and remind yourself that you aren't *settling*. You need to find someone who values and appreciates you. Remember, you're moving forward, not just treading water.

Recognize Your Positive Steps

You're learning to listen to your instincts and to believe in your own capacity to build a new life for yourself. Recognizing your worth as a human being and a woman is important to your growth. Set goals that reflect that philosophy. You're making progress if you are happy with the state of your social life—dating if you want to be, or not dating if that's what you want. In addition, be proud of yourself if you've set some ground rules for upcoming holidays that reinforce the fact that you're trying to build a new life for yourself (and your children, if you have any) away from your ex.

- **You're not ready to date someone else if:**
  - You're acting out of your fear that no one else will want you.
  - You're still saying negative things about yourself without challenging them.
- **You're ready to date someone else if:**
  - You recognize that while dating can be difficult, you have a lot to offer.
  - You're ready to move on with your life and find a relationship that's more positive.

Exercises and Affirmations

Be daring! Get on a dating site and answer some lucky guy's ad. It doesn't have to be magic between you. This is a *date*, not a marriage proposal. Nothing may come of it, but you can still get out and exercise your dating muscles. Enjoy being with a guy and live in the moment.

When you walk through the grocery store or the mall, look people in the face and smile. Or, strike up a conversation with someone in the elevator at work. This will probably surprise them, but it'll help you learn to casually interact. After all, the floor lights above the elevator door aren't that interesting.

When you lie down to sleep at night, repeat this mantra: "I may not always *feel* good, but that doesn't mean I'm *not* good. I can do this life!"

Conclusion

Moving Forward!

It's my hope that the exercises and suggestions in this book have helped you reach a decision and encouraged you to learn about yourself.

If you've decided to stay in your relationship and work together on the issues, give yourself credit for making the effort. No one should ever be ashamed of *not* leaving, no matter what friends and relatives say. Whether or not you need to leave is truly your own decision. Doing what's best for you needs to be your goal.

Give yourself permission to talk about your needs and your desires. It's as important as listening to your partner's. Both you and your partner have to be invested to make a relationship work.

This relationship decision is a great opportunity to examine your life and find out what works for you. Every suggestion in this book has had that aim.

Relationships require big effort and need to have big rewards. You deserve a happy life with a mate who works as hard as you do to keep the relationship healthy.

Leaving a relationship is a very personal choice. No one lives in your relationship like you do. They don't know it the way you do. This is your life, and you're the one who deals with the consequences of your choices—so you, therefore, get to make those choices.

Expect yourself to make mistakes. You can't be perfect; it's not possible. Trying with all your might to avoid mistakes just leaves you paralyzed. Besides, we learn from our mistakes; they're not meaningless.

You're living your life. That's the bravest act of all!

Index